THE STORY OF THE CHURCH

From Pentecost to Modern Times

WORKBOOK

WITH ANSWER KEY

ISBN: 978-1-5051-1665-6

Published in the United States by
TAN Books
P.O. Box 269
Gastonia, NC 28053
www.TANBooks.com

Printed and bound in the United States of America

A Word to the Teacher

Using This Workbook

TAN Books' *The Story of the Church* follows the immensely popular and successful series *The Story of the Bible* and *The Story of Civilization*. While there are some similarities between these, *The Story of the Church* breaks from the other two in several ways, beginning with this student workbook.

While *The Story of the Bible* and *The Story of Civilization* were targeted to younger students, *The Story of the Church* is targeted to middle schoolers. By this point, they should have a firm grasp of both world history and Bible history and be prepared to tackle the history of Holy Mother Church. Yes, there will be some crossover with the content—that is only natural since our programs present history through the faithful prism of the Church—but this text goes deeper into Church history, developing more complete pictures of the popes, saints, councils, encyclicals, and spiritual movements that have helped Christ's Church blossom throughout the world.

With all this in mind, this workbook takes a different approach from the supplemental material in past *Story of* series, which consisted of activity books for younger students filled with all sorts of coloring pages, arts and crafts, and games. Since this workbook is targeted to middle schoolers, much of the content will consist of multiple choice, matching, true/false, fill in the blank, and a host of writing exercises and essays meant to provoke deeper thought in the students. That being said, we don't want to make this *all* work, so there will be some crossword puzzles, word searches, and double puzzles.

The general pattern for each chapter is one exercise meant to test the student's knowledge of the chapter, along with one exercise that is more fun or something that engenders more free thought. We recommend doing both exercises from each chapter, but a teacher knows what is best for his or her students, so be as flexible as you like. If you do complete both exercises in each chapter, it should take 20–40 minutes. If you include reading the chapter itself for 20–30 minutes, this means each chapter should be about an hour of work.

Lastly, for any exercise that has objective answers, you will find those answers in the back (responses for subjective exercises and essays will obviously vary from student to student). Since the workbook is perforated, tear out each chapter's content and give it to your student, then use the answer key in the back to grade it. For the written exercises, feel free to use the space provided or have your student use a computer or separate journal.

Thank you for taking the time to educate the next generation about the history of Holy Mother Church!

TAN Books

CHAPTER 1
Christ and the Apostles

Short Answer

Answer the following questions in a few complete sentences.

1. Explain the story of Pentecost. What happened? Why is this seen as the birth of the Church?

2. What does the word *apostle* mean? Even though you are not a successor of the apostles (a bishop), how are you called to fulfill the role of an apostle of Christ?

3. Go back into your Bible and read the story of the Tower of Babel (Genesis 11:1–9). How does this story seem related, but in an opposite sense, to Pentecost?

4. Who were the *presbyters* in the early Church?

5. List a few interesting facts about St. Paul.

Crossword Puzzle

Across

3. The Holy Spirit appeared to the disciples and Mary as ________ of fire.
6. An office created to help minister to the needs of the sick and poor
7. The first priests
8. St. Paul was traveling to the city of ________ when Christ appeared to him.

Down

1. The only apostle not to suffer a martyr's death
2. Seen as the birth of the Church
4. The place where Pentecost took place
5. Roman Emperor who blamed the great fire of Rome on the Christians
7. St. John was exiled to the island of ________.
9. St. Paul's original name

CHAPTER 2
The Apostolic Age

Multiple Choice

Pick the best answer.

1. The word *evangelist* comes from the Greek work *evangel*, meaning:

A. good news.
B. bad news.
C. spreading news.
D. holy words.

2. According to tradition, which one of the four Gospel writers was the secretary of St. Peter?

A. Matthew
B. Mark
C. Luke
D. John

3. This place was where Jews read from the Scriptures and worshiped God.

A. church
B. synagogue
C. tabernacle
D. temple

4. The passing on of the powers of the Apostles to each successive generation of bishops is known as:

A. transubstantiation.
B. apostolic anointing.
C. pentecostal passing.
D. apostolic succession.

5. This early Church saint is often depicted holding an anchor because of the way he was martyred.

A. Polycarp
B. Ignatius
C. Clement
D. Paul

Word Search

Find the hidden words from chapter 2. For extra work, consider writing down something you read in the text about each person, place, or term you find.

Apostolic age, tradition, Ignatius, Thessalonians, Polycarp, universal, bishops, Luke

Note: Some words may appear backwards.

CHAPTER 3
The Apologists

Writing Assignment: A Catholic "Apology"

Use the space provided or type it up on your computer.

After reading the chapter on Christian apologists, try your own effort at it. Pretend a non-Catholic friend approaches you and asks why you "worship" Mary and why you think the Eucharist is truly the Body of Christ and not a symbol. Write a short response to both these common objections Catholics often hear today.

Writing Assignment: Acrostic Poem

Use the space provided or type it up on your computer.

In the space below, write the name Justin vertically, in reference to St. Justin Martyr, and create an acrostic poem. Using each letter in his name, state a fact or something interesting about St. Justin that you read about in the text. The sentence can start with that letter or the letter can be found at any point in the sentence.

CHAPTER 4
Roman Persecutions

Matching

Match each term with the statement or phrase that describes it.

A. persecution
B. genius
C. Nero
D. apostatize
E. *Libellus*
F. Agatha
G. Valerian
H. Lawrence

_____ 1. like a guardian spirit of a Roman household

_____ 2. Roman emperor who persecuted Christians

_____ 3. an early Christian martyr who took a vow of virginity

_____ 4. hostility and ill-treatment of a group of people

_____ 5. a certificate which proved you had sacrificed to the Roman gods

_____ 6. a Roman deacon burned alive

_____ 7. persecuted Christians after the Great Fire of Rome in AD 64

_____ 8. to denounce your faith publicly

Writing Assignment: Short Story

Use the space provided or type it up on your computer.

Take some time to write your own short story, about the same length as the one in the text, about an early Christian martyr. You can write about a well-known saint or an ordinary citizen that you make up. Describe the scene and their courage.

CHAPTER 5
Dissent and Heresy

Multiple Choice

Pick the best answer.

1. What did the Church Father Tertullian say was the seed of the Church?

A. the sacraments
B. the Gospel
C. the blood of the martyrs
D. the faith of the martyrs

2. Heresy is:

A. a myth or story told to convey a difficult teaching.
B. a false teaching about Jesus Christ and the truths he revealed.
C. gossiping about others.
D. condemning Christians who preach about Jesus.

3. What did the heresy of Gnosticism claim?

A. that Jesus not did really take flesh in the womb of Mary
B. that the God of the Old Testament was different from the God of the New Testament
C. that Jesus was only part-man and part-God, rather than fully human and fully divine
D. that matter and the whole material world were evil, and only spiritual things were good; therefore God, because he is good, could not have created the material world

4. Which of the following saints was an outspoken opponent of Arianism?

A. St. Augustine
B. St. Athanasius
C. St. Benedict
D. St. Tertullian

5. Orthodoxy means:

A. correct thinking.
B. honest thinking.
C. faithful thinking.
D. heretical thinking.

Double Puzzle

Unscramble the words below from chapter 5. Copy the letters in the numbered blocks to the blocks with the corresponding numbers at the bottom to help answer the question.

NIAUHTASSA (block 3)

TEICERH (block 2)

EGSUUATNI (block 4)

DITNOSSTA (block 1)

SOITGMCNIS (block 5)

DOHROOTXY

FEDNEEDR

The Arian heresy was named after this man:

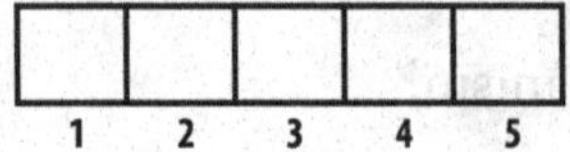

CHAPTER 6
Christian Monasticism

Short Answer

Answer the following questions in a few complete sentences.

1. Describe the kind of life St. Paul the Hermit lived.

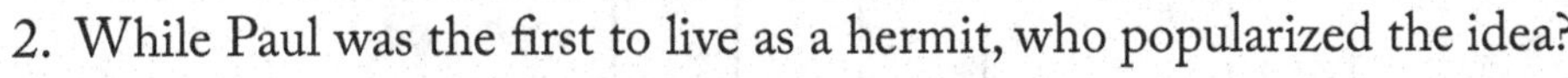

2. While Paul was the first to live as a hermit, who popularized the idea?

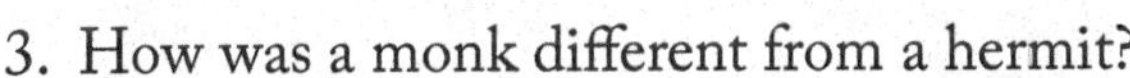

3. How was a monk different from a hermit?

4. How do we know about the life of St. Anthony if he lived such a private life and lived so long ago?

5. Who were the Stylites?

Crossword Puzzle

Across

3. A person who lives completely on his own, seeking a closer relationship with God by living in solitude
6. Gave away a large inheritance to become a hermit
7. Known as the first Christian hermit
9. A way of life where people give up worldly pursuits to focus on seeking God

Down

1. Attacked Anthony on many occasions
2. A disciple of St. Anthony
4. "Pillar Saints"
5. A place where hermits often lived
8. Like hermits but lived together in communities

CHAPTER 7
The Triumph of the Church

Matching

Match each term with the statement or phrase that describes it.

A. St. Sebastian
B. Diocletian
C. Augustus
D. Sol Invictus
E. Council of Nicaea
F. Caesar
G. Galerius
H. Christendom
I. St. Helen
J. Constantine

_____ 1. The Roman Sun god

_____ 2. Successor to the Augustus

_____ 3. A time, lasting over a thousand years, when culture and politics were shaped by the Catholic faith

_____ 4. Roman emperor who issued a decree of persecutions against the Christians in the year 303

_____ 5. Mother of Constantine

_____ 6. The Church's first Ecumenical Council

_____ 7. Was shot with arrows and martyred during the persecution of Diocletian

_____ 8. Roman emperor who converted to Christianity; issued the Edict of Milan

_____ 9. Co-emperor with Diocletian who ruled the West

_____10. Name the Roman emperors called themselves

Writing Assignment: Make a List

Use the space provided or type it up on your computer.

In this chapter, you read about the Council of Nicaea, where they promulgated the Nicene Creed, which was a statement about what they believed as Christians at that time. Without looking at the Creed, make a list of the major things we believe as Catholics. When you are finished, go look at the Nicene Creed and come back to see how many you got, and how many you left off.

CHAPTER 8
The Benedictines

True or False?

In the blank beside each statement, write "T" if the statement is True or "F" if the statement is False. If the statement is False, change it to make it true. Either write a new statement in the margins or mark up the sentence itself.

_____ 1. After the Roman Empire became Christian, nothing but good things happened there.

_____ 2. St. Benedict wrote the book *City of God.*

_____ 3. St. Augustine is a Doctor of the Church.

_____ 4. St. Benedict was from Italy.

_____ 5. St. Benedict came from a poor family and had no education.

_____ 6. The abbot is the head of a monastery.

_____ 7. St. Benedict founded his first monastery at Monte Cassino where Apollo was once worshiped.

_____ 8. St. Benedict's motto, *ora et labora*, means "fast and prayer."

_____ 9. The *Rule of St. Benedict* said many things about how a monastery ought to be run.

_____10. Every monk who lived under St. Benedict loved and respected him.

Writing Assignment: Write Your Own "Rule"

St. Benedict composed the *Rule of St. Benedict,* or the Benedictine Rule, which divided the day into periods of prayer, study, work, and rest. His motto was *ora et labora*, "prayer and work." Benedict believed monks should keep busy with their hands, whether copying manuscripts or working in the monastery's orchard or some other form of work. The *Rule of St. Benedict* said many things about how a monastery ought to be run.

Jot down a list of rules for your own home, either ones already in place or ones you would like to put in place. How could your home be run to draw your family closer to God?

CHAPTER 9
A Time of Missionaries

Multiple Choice

Pick the best answer.

1. Which of the following countries has the distinction of being the first Christian nation?

A. England
B. Armenia
C. Spain
D. France

2. Who founded the first convent in Ireland?

A. St. Patrick
B. St. Enda
C. St. Brigid
D. St. Clotilde

3. Who was the Christian princess married to Clovis who helped convert him, leading France to become the first pagan kingdom within the boundaries of the old Roman Empire to embrace the Catholic faith?

A. St. Columba
B. St. Enda
C. St. Brigid
D. St. Clotilde

4. Two saintly brothers, St. Isidore and St. Leander, helped convert the Visigoth tribes of this nation to the Catholic faith.

A. England
B. Armenia
C. Spain
D. France

5. The Anglo-Saxon pagans that St. Augustine of Canterbury converted were inhabitants of what modern day country?

A. England
B. Armenia
C. Spain
D. France

Writing Assignment: Converting the Nations

Write a few sentences for each nation listed below detailing how their people came to accept the Catholic faith.

Armenia:

Ireland:

France:

Spain:

England:

CHAPTER 10
Rome and the Byzantines

Matching

Match each term with the statement or phrase that describes it.

A. *Regula Pastoralis*
B. Mohammed
C. excommunicated
D. Islam
E. iconoclasm
F. Gregorian chant
G. Pope St. Gregory I

_____ 1. founder of Islam

_____ 2. a book written by Pope St. Gregory I on how to be a good bishop

_____ 3. a heresy that said Christians should not venerate images

_____ 4. to be removed from the Church and deprived of the sacraments

_____ 5. a type of singing named after Pope St. Gregory I

_____ 6. wrote the first biography of St. Benedict

_____ 7. means "submission"

Word Search

Find the hidden words from chapter 10. For extra work, consider writing down something you read in the text about each person, place, or term you find.

Islam, Pope Gregory, excommunicated, icon, Emperor Leo, Gregorian chant, Allah, Mecca

E	A	H	G	A	C	M	E	G	G	P	A	T	D	B
H	X	V	C	F	A	B	E	V	R	V	A	G	X	V
J	J	C	F	H	H	W	E	Y	E	S	R	T	N	N
A	E	T	O	R	U	L	C	C	G	P	H	J	D	U
M	A	V	J	M	N	S	I	J	O	I	A	L	E	D
L	Q	C	B	T	M	E	N	P	R	Y	L	X	E	E
H	J	T	S	W	C	U	E	H	I	G	L	I	X	Q
C	L	W	M	Y	W	G	N	D	A	Z	A	M	Y	F
E	T	U	W	A	R	N	W	I	N	C	C	R	I	P
L	L	R	M	E	L	B	B	X	C	B	Y	A	P	L
L	T	V	G	T	C	S	I	S	H	A	J	O	I	Y
N	X	O	Z	V	D	E	I	X	A	F	T	Y	C	L
E	R	T	B	V	G	Y	N	L	N	T	O	E	J	C
Y	P	D	T	U	Y	C	F	T	T	M	K	R	D	N
O	E	L	R	O	R	E	P	M	E	I	C	O	N	W

Note: Some words may appear backwards.

CHAPTER 11
The Carolingians

Short Answer

Answer the following questions in a few complete sentences.

1. Who was Charles Martel and why was he considered a hero?

2. How did Pepin the Short, Charles Martel's son, overthrow the Merovingians to become king of the Franks?

3. How did the Papal States come to be?

4. Write down what you know about Charlemagne.

5. Retell the story of St. Boniface and the great oak tree.

Crossword Puzzle

Across

3. Modern day name for the kingdom of the Franks
5. St. Boniface chopped it down
7. Defeated the Moors at Tours
8. Pope Leo III crowned Charlemagne on this day
9. Was a short leader

Down

1. Means "Charles the Great"
2. Pope who helped Pepin become king of the Franks
4. Land owned by the popes
6. A document issued by the pope about some important matter

CHAPTER 12
Dark Days for the Papacy

True or False?

In the blank beside each statement, write "T" if the statement is True or "F" if the statement is False. If the statement is False, change it to make it true. Either write a new statement in the margins or mark up the sentence itself.

____ 1. The Church and the Carolingians both benefited from their alliance.

____ 2. Pope Stephen put Pope Formosus on trial just before he died.

____ 3. Lay investiture was when a new bishop was invested with the symbols of his office by the ruler, who was a layman.

____ 4. Otto the Great originally came from Italy.

____ 5. Crowning Otto as Holy Roman emperor worked out well for Pope John XII.

____ 6. An antipope is a term given to a bad pope.

____ 7. Other kingdoms outside of the Holy Roman Empire, such as England and France, began to practice lay investiture.

____ 8. The practice of clergymen getting involved in politics was bad for the Church.

Double Puzzle

Unscramble the words below from chapter 12. Copy the letters in the numbered blocks to the blocks with the corresponding numbers at the bottom to help answer the question.

The name given to the trial where one pope put a deceased pope on trial.

TOTO — 4 blocks (block 4 numbered 11)

ALY VINISERTEUT — 3 blocks (block 3 numbered 9) + 11 blocks (block 1 numbered 10, block 4 numbered 6)

RGCAEHMLEAM — 11 blocks (block 1 numbered 1)

RAENMYG — 7 blocks (block 5 numbered 2)

NEAPIOPT — 8 blocks (block 1 numbered 4)

NEANLDG — 7 blocks (block 7 numbered 3)

SOIHPSB — 7 blocks (block 3 numbered 8)

RTEBI RERVI — 5 blocks (block 5 numbered 7) + 5 blocks (block 3 numbered 5)

The name given to the trial where one pope put a deceased pope on trial.

1	2	3	4	5	6	7

8	9	10	11	3

CHAPTER 13
The Struggle Against Lay Authority

Multiple Choice

Pick the best answer.

1. The practice of simony is:

A. holding a priest or bishop hostage.
B. buying and selling Church offices.
C. allowing priests to marry.
D. politically influencing papal elections.

2. Which of the following is *not* true about the Cluny monastery?

A. St. Berno was its first abbot.
B. It inspired reforms within the Church.
C. The man who built the monastery regarded it as his own personal property.
D. It helped end lay dominance of the Church.

3. This pope popularized the process of the cardinals electing the pope.

A. Berno
B. Pius III
C. Pope Henry
D. Gregory VII

4. How did Henry IV get back into the good graces of Pope Gregory VII after Gregory excommunicated him?

A. He gave him lots of money and treasure.
B. He built him a cathedral.
C. He begged for forgiveness while kneeling in the snow.
D. He killed the pope's rivals.

5. What is a concordat?

A. an agreement between the Church and the government of a nation
B. a statement of excommunication on a king
C. a peace treaty between nations
D. a warrant for someone's arrest

6. What were the reforms called that intended to restrict the influence of the pope in England and curb the power of bishops there?

A. Penal Laws
B. Constitutions of Clarendon
C. Constitutions of Concordat
D. Anti-Clerical Constitutions

7. Where was Thomas Becket the bishop?

A. Canterbury
B. Worms
C. London
D. Clarendon

8. How was Thomas Becket killed?

A. King Henry had his head chopped off.
B. King Henry stabbed him.
C. King Henry crucified him.
D. King Henry's knights killed him after believing Henry wanted him dead.

Writing Assignment: A Letter to the President

Use the space provided or use your computer.

Imagine that the president of the United States, with the approval of Congress, passes a law that says the US government will begin to appoint the Catholic Church's bishops and cardinals within the United States. Write a letter to the president explaining why you think this is a horrible law and give your reasons why. Consider referencing the historical issues the Church faced in the past over this very matter.

CHAPTER 14
The Crusading Ideal

Matching

Match each term with the statement or phrase that describes it.

A. Constantinople
B. schism
C. Michael Cerularius
D. Hagia Sophia
E. East-West Schism
F. Seljuk Turks
G. Crusade
H. indulgence
I. the Church
J. military order
K. Knights of the Temple
L. pilgrimage

____ 1. term for the separation of the Eastern and Western churches

____ 2. Islamic conquerors who sparked the first crusade

____ 3. famous basilica of the Byzantine Empire

____ 4. a journey taken for a spiritual purpose

____ 5. means "cross-bearer"

____ 6. to break communion with the Church

____ 7. a band of knights who took religious vows; "fighting monks"

____ 8. Byzantine patriarch who angered Pope Leo IX

____ 9. capital of the Byzantine Empire

____ 10. Jerusalem from above

____ 11. known as the Templars

____ 12. a cancellation of penance for sins already confessed

Word Search

Find the hidden words from chapter 14. For extra work, consider writing down something you read in the text about each person, place, or term you find.

Crusade, Templars, penance, schism, indulgence, Turks, Constantinople, Hospitallers, Byzantine, Hagia Sophia

E	I	N	Y	A	G	W	S	C	T	C	H	E	F	X
M	C	T	E	N	J	R	C	U	K	O	J	N	G	J
E	R	N	C	W	A	Q	R	M	S	N	G	I	A	S
B	P	M	E	L	Q	K	I	P	N	S	B	T	H	V
E	G	E	P	G	S	B	I	I	K	T	Q	N	S	Y
V	R	M	N	T	L	T	E	K	B	A	H	A	C	R
C	E	W	M	A	A	U	G	V	P	N	Z	Z	H	C
T	P	J	I	L	N	F	D	D	R	T	H	Y	I	C
G	B	C	L	Y	C	C	M	N	A	I	T	B	S	G
P	F	E	W	D	K	T	E	V	I	N	U	B	M	A
H	R	C	R	U	S	A	D	E	U	O	G	H	I	K
S	I	L	Z	F	B	G	Y	O	N	P	L	R	T	H
N	O	B	S	L	N	I	Q	S	T	L	P	G	W	R
B	H	T	I	H	H	R	M	H	U	E	E	J	Y	F
A	I	H	P	O	S	A	I	G	A	H	C	C	G	V

Note: Some words may appear backwards.

CHAPTER 15
Monastic Reform Movements

True or False?

In the blank beside each statement, write "T" if the statement is True or "F" if the statement is False. If the statement is False, change it to make it true. Either write a new statement in the margins or mark up the sentence itself.

____ 1. During the period of growth for religious orders, there were new orders founded but also reforms made to existing orders.

____ 2. St. Norbert of Xanten was originally a poor man who became a monk, continuing to live in poverty after taking his vows.

____ 3. The Premonstratensians—or Norbertines—used a version of the monastic rule written by St. Benedict.

____ 4. A *double monastery* is a two-story monastery.

____ 5. A *Third Order* is a branch of a religious order open to lay persons.

____ 6. Robert of Molesme left his first monastery because it had too much money, relaxing the strict life of the monks.

____ 7. St. Bernard of Clairvaux founded many Norbertine monasteries.

____ 8. By the time St. Bernard died in 1153, the Cistercian Order was the fastest growing religious order in Europe.

____ 9. The Carthusians devoted much of their time to copying religious manuscripts.

____ 10. St. Elizabeth was the queen of Norway.

Crossword Puzzle

Across

3. St. Bernard of __________
6. Founded the Carthusians
7. German mystic
8. Another name for the Norbertines
9. St. Elizabeth came from this country

Down

1. A monastery where monks and nuns live under one roof but in separate wings
2. Founded the Norbertines
4. A branch of a religious order open to lay persons
5. Helped her husband, the Scottish king, grow in virtue

CHAPTER 16
The Mendicant Orders

Short Answer

Answer the following questions in a few complete sentences.

1. Though things were mostly going well for Christendom by the year 1200, what were some of the issues facing the Church?

2. What was Francis like before turning his life toward God?

3. Explain what happened during and after Francis's famous vision of Christ in the old, ruined chapel of San Damiano near Assisi.

4. Why was Francis's order called a "mendicant" order?

5. How did Francis ultimately receive approval for his Franciscan order?

Writing Assignment: Why the Rosary is so important

In the space provided or on your computer, write a short essay explaining why you like to pray the Rosary and why you find this prayer so important to your spiritual life and the life of the Church. How would you explain why you pray the Rosary to someone who has never heard of it? Consider including a history of how the Rosary came to be and how St. Dominic used it to defeat heresies.

CHAPTER 17
Scholasticism

Multiple Choice

Pick the best answer.

1. Scholasticism comes from the Latin word for school; it essentially means:

A. education of the schoolmen.
B. philosophy of the schoolmen.
C. teaching of the people.
D. learning of the people.

2. After the fall of the Roman Empire, most education took place:

A. in schools.
B. in castles.
C. in monasteries.
D. in the fields.

3. Which of the following was *not* considered one of the seven liberal arts?

A. grammar
B. music
C. arithmetic
D. public speaking

4. What was the primary purpose of the medieval universities?

A. providing education to glorify God
B. bringing together students and teachers
C. passing along of knowledge
D. All of the above.

5. What was the document given by the pope called which gave a university independence from any bishop or lord?

A. charter
B. pledge
C. note
D. declaration

6. Which of the following cities was *not* a site of one of the first major universities?

A. Paris (France)
B. Dublin (Ireland)
C. Oxford (England)
D. Bologna (Italy)

7. What is the primary difference between philosophy and theology?

A. Only priests can study theology, whereas anyone can study philosophy.
B. Philosophy was a pagan activity and theology a Christian one.
C. Theology is the study of the revealed truths of the Christian faith, while philosophy is the study of general truths known by reason alone.
D. There is no difference between the two; they are basically synonyms.

8. The introduction of this Greek philosopher's ideas into the Latin speaking West changed the way people thought about philosophy and how it related to faith.

A. Aristotle
B. Socrates
C. Plato
D. Homer

9. What religious order was St. Thomas Aquinas a part of?

A. Benedictines
B. Dominicans
C. Norbertines
D. Carmelites

10. What was the name of St. Thomas's famous literary work that shapes so much of the Church's theology today?

A. *The Rule of St. Thomas*
B. *The Theology of Everything*
C. *The Summa Theologiae*
D. *The Philosophy of the Schoolmen*

Double Puzzle

Unscramble the words below from chapter 17. Copy the letters in the numbered blocks to the blocks with the corresponding numbers at the bottom to help answer the question.

QUNSAIA

14 16 5

TEARIOTLS

1

RTHECRA

10

VURNYIIEST

6 18

POPLYHHOSI

17 8

HYOLOGTE

12

SAMMU

3

TIISSCMSOCHAL

9 13

TESMONRAY

11 15 2

BNRUENETVAU

7 4

The theological word the Church uses to describe how the bread and wine of the Eucharist turn into the Body and Blood of Christ at Mass.

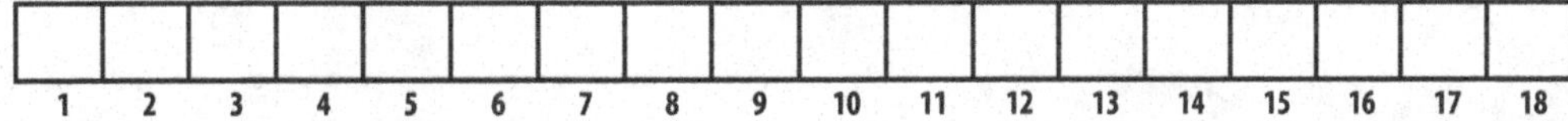

1 2 3 4 5 6 7 8 9 10 11 12 13 14 15 16 17 18

CHAPTER 18
Kings Versus Popes

Matching

Match each term with the statement or phrase that describes it.

A. Gelasius	E. Third Crusade	I. *Unam Sanctam*
B. Investiture Controversy	F. Frederick II	J. Jacques de Molay
C. Frederick Barbarossa	G. King Edward I	K. *Clericos Laicos*
D. Alexander III	H. Boniface VIII	

____ 1. pope attacked by King Philip's thugs

____ 2. declared clergy who refused to pay taxes to their king outlaws

____ 3. papal bull prohibiting the taxation and stealing of the Church's goods to pay for war

____ 4. grandmaster of the Templar Knights, arrested by King Philip

____ 5. excommunicated Emperor Frederick for his support of the antipope

____ 6. German king who became Holy Roman emperor

____ 7. the Church called him the Antichrist

____ 8. the attempt to reclaim the Kingdom of Jerusalem from the Muslims

____ 9. an argument over how much control the Holy Roman Empire should have over the Church

____ 10. pope who wrote about the separation of Church and State

____ 11. papal bull that taught kings were not exempt from the duty of listening to the pope

Writing Assignment: Church and State

Recall the Scripture passage: "Render therefore to Caesar the things that are Caesar's and to God the things that are God's" (Mt 22:21). In the space provided or on your computer, write a short essay explaining what this means. How should we balance our life between our relationship with God and within our civic community?

CHAPTER 19
The Babylonian Captivity

True or False?

In the blank beside each statement, write "T" if the statement is True or "F" if the statement is False. If the statement is False, change it to make it true. Either write a new statement in the margins or mark up the sentence itself.

____ 1. When the cardinals met to elect a new pope in 1305, they sought the advice of King Philip IV.

____ 2. Clement V was a French pope who basically allowed King Philip to do whatever he wanted.

____ 3. Even though Clement was a French pope, he wanted to live in Rome.

____ 4. Most Catholics liked the papal court being moved to France.

____ 5. Seven popes across sixty-seven years lived in Avignon and away from Rome.

____ 6. The time of the Avignon papacy was referred to as the Babylonian Captivity.

____ 7. One of the favorite pastimes of Christians during the 1300s was going to see plays with religious themes.

____ 8. Mummers plays featured two characters who fell in love.

____ 9. In Everyman plays, a character would be reminded of his duties to God, often through an encounter with Death.

____ 10. St. Catherine of Siena was a mystic and holy woman who played at least a small role in the papacy returning to Rome.

Word Search

Find the hidden words from chapter 19. For extra work, consider writing down something you read in the text about each person, place, or term you find.

Everyman, Catherine, Clement, Philip, Avignon, Mummers, Boniface, Babylonian, Captivity

J H G W L R M F C K W Q V R V O N D Y

X B F F K I R L C E A V D W V A U T M

T O F V W L E B T W E P C H X X I D M

L N D Z Q M G W N G E L C N K V Z F L

Z I C H E Z I M B G B D Z H I Z I U A

O F M N R G L Q J C F Q Q T R O G W A

R A T N O N G I V A Y F P C O F P G E

F C J Z H I V O E Z S A H G L Z N E M

U E K Q R O K D Z V C R L T L L F W S

T E Y F P Z M R W N E H E P Q O B P A

G G P U A U M Y A L C R Y M O X J I N

Y W L R H J M I E I U T Y E M L R L V

V T A D G W N S G N L F E M W U K I N

D O Y K F O K H U W C J N Y A H M H U

I P L E L X X L P O K U K U Y N W P H

E Z N Y C A T H E R I N E K T T Z A I

C V B E H H H T L D B V I K V B O M N

K A P G O I U F P X I W B L Y J N F N

B N W I A R V H R J A G N U U X C W Q

Note: Some words may appear backwards.

CHAPTER 20
The Great Western Schism

Short Answer

Answer the following questions in a few complete sentences.

1. What happened after Gregory XI—the pope who returned the papal court to Rome—died?

2. What was the Great Western Schism?

3. What did the Great Western Schism do to the Church?

4. What happened at the Council of Pisa in 1409? What was the point of this council?

5. In the end, who do people believe the real pope was during the Great Western Schism?

Writing Assignment – The Importance of the Church's Unity

Write a short essay in the space provided or on your computer about the importance of the Church's unity. Why is it so vital for the Church to be *one*? What problems arise when two men (or more) claim to be pope? Imagine if that happened today. What sort of problems do you think would arise, including practical ones?

CHAPTER 21
Late Medieval Mysticism

Multiple Choice

Pick the best answer.

1. Mysticism refers to:

A. the aspect of the Christian faith which focuses on conditioning the soul to be transformed by the grace of God.
B. the part of Catholic spirituality that dwells on the inner life of the soul.
C. how God reveals himself to people interiorly.
D. all of the above.

2. Which of the following does NOT describe a mystic?

A. someone who cultivates his interior life
B. someone who must be a clergyman
C. someone chosen by God for special graces
D. someone who often lives in seclusion

3. Which of the following brought about a growing interest in mysticism?

A. the visions of Our Lady of Lourdes
B. an increase in exorcisms
C. People were becoming better educated and books were more readily available, leading many to concern themselves with their personal salvation.
D. The Church began to teach more about the mystics of centuries past.

4. One of the most popular devotional books of the Middle Ages was:

A. *The Imitation of Christ.*
B. *Mystical Visions of the Middle Ages.*
C. the *Summa.*
D. the *Catechism.*

5. A man who lived in perpetual enclosure in a cell or room from which they never departed was called a:

A. monk.
B. anchorite.
C. Beghard.
D. anchoress.

6. From what country did the Beguines and Beghards emerge?

A. France
B. Sweden
C. the Netherlands
D. Italy

7. The famous book Julian of Norwich wrote where she chronicled her visions of Jesus and other mystical visions was called:

A. *The Visions of Julian of Norwich.*
B. *Revelations of Divine Love.*
C. *Revelations of Julian of Norwich.*
D. *The Spiritual Espousals.*

8. Why was *The Book of Margery Kempe* so famous?

A. It is considered the first autobiography in the English language.
B. It was the first English book written by a woman.
C. It chronicled the first approved Marian apparition.
D. It predicted when the end of the world would come.

Crossword Puzzle

Across

3. English city where St. Julian came from
5. A woman who lives in perpetual enclosure
6. Wrote *Revelations of Divine Love*
8. Wrote *Imitation of Christ*

Down

1. A man who lives in perpetual enclosure
2. Made books more readily available
4. Chosen by God for special graces and gifts
7. German mystic who inspired lay people to holiness

CHAPTER 22
The Outbreak of Protestantism

Matching

Match each term with the statement or phrase that describes it.

A. John Calvin
B. Charles V
C. Albigensians
D. Protestants
E. annulment
F. John Fisher
G. presbyters
H. indulgence
I. simony
J. Anne Boleyn
K. Lollards
L. Jan Hus
M. Martin Luther
N. Henry VIII
O. French Wars of Religion
P. predestination

____ 1. A decree declaring a marriage to be invalid, thus allowing one to remarry

____ 2. Groups of elders

____ 3. States that God decides from all eternity who will go to heaven and who will go to hell

____ 4. Author of *Institutes of the Christian Religion*

____ 5. Leader of the Hussites who wanted Church property taken away and to force the Church to live in poverty

____ 6. The buying or selling of spiritual things

____ 7. Holy Roman emperor who fought back against the Lutheran rebels

____ 8. King of England and founder of Anglicanism

____ 9. Preached that the flesh was evil and the human body was created by an evil spirit and only the soul was from God

____ 10. Henry VIII's mistress

____ 11. Huguenots and Catholics battling for control of the French throne

____ 12. Rejected many of the Church's traditions, taught the Bible alone was the sole rule of faith, and that the Eucharist was not truly the body and blood of Christ

____ 13. Martyred under Henry VIII

____ 14. A cancellation of penance for sins already confessed

____ 15. German Augustinian friar who wrote the *95 Theses*

____ 16. Those who opposed the Catholic Church; comes from the word *protest*

Writing Assignment – Characters of the Reformation

In the space provided below, write a short summary of each character of the Protestant Reformation. While these are not the only important figures, they are three of the most prominent. Explain where they come from, their background, and how they spread heresy and divided the Church.

Martin Luther

John Calvin

King Henry VIII

CHAPTER 23
Trent and the Counter-Reformation

True or False?

In the blank beside each statement, write "T" if the statement is True or "F" if the statement is False. If the statement is False, change it to make it true. Either write a new statement in the margins or mark up the sentence itself.

____ 1. The Protestant Reformation takes its name because the Protestants thought they were "reforming" the Church.

____ 2. The Protestant revolt marked a turning point from which Christendom has not yet recovered.

____ 3. Henry VIII had always been an enemy of the Church.

____ 4. Pope Paul III summoned the Council of Trent in response to the Protestant Reformation.

____ 5. The purpose of the Council of Trent was to devise a military strategy to take down the Protestants.

____ 6. Seminaries were places where priests gathered to pray.

____ 7. The movement of spirituality and art that followed the Council of Trent is often called the Counter-Reformation.

____ 8. Cardinal Charles Borromeo founded the first seminary in Rome.

____ 9. There were many martyrs during the Reformation and the period following it.

____ 10. Art was an important aspect of the Counter-Reformation.

Double Puzzle

Unscramble the words below from chapter 23. Copy the letters in the numbered blocks to the blocks with the corresponding numbers at the bottom to help answer the question.

TEURONC-TOONAFRERMI ☐☐☐☐☐☐☐ - ☐☐☐☐☐☐☐☐☐☐☐ (3, 2)

SESIRMIANE ☐☐☐☐☐☐☐☐☐☐ (1)

NERTT ☐☐☐☐☐ (6)

OEPP LUAP ☐☐☐☐ ☐☐☐☐ (7)

SALEHRC BEOMRROO ☐☐☐☐☐☐☐ ☐☐☐☐☐☐☐☐ (9)

CSSITVAILN ☐☐☐☐☐☐☐☐☐☐ (8)

NIAML ☐☐☐☐☐

VAARACGOGI ☐☐☐☐☐☐☐☐☐☐

CIHANLABD ☐☐☐☐☐☐☐☐☐ (5)

RIINEBN ☐☐☐☐☐☐☐ (4)

The Capuchin friar and theologian who was sent to preach among the Calvinists of Switzerland to bring them back to the faith, but was eventually martyred.

☐☐ . ☐☐☐☐☐☐☐

1 2 . 3 4 5 6 7 8 9

CHAPTER 24
The Jesuits

Short Answer

Answer the following questions in a few complete sentences.

1. List a few things you read about St. Ignatius.

2. What was Ignatius's goal in writing his *Exercises*?

3. List a few things you read about the Jesuits.

4. What were the Penal Laws and what was the history behind them?

5. How did English Catholics respond to the Penal Laws?

Word Search

Find the hidden words from chapter 24. For extra work, consider writing down something you read in the text about each person, place, or term you find.

Ignatius, Page, Jesuits, Francis Xavier, Penal Laws, Elizabeth, missionary, Spiritual Exercises

F	N	S	C	E	C	T	I	G	X	P	M	D	N	W	K	G	R
B	R	B	U	U	O	E	Q	K	B	D	V	Y	H	A	P	R	L
X	Z	A	K	I	S	W	I	I	O	X	O	N	H	U	Z	K	T
M	Y	R	N	K	T	D	G	F	P	J	J	T	Z	S	S	W	K
G	I	O	V	C	P	A	Q	R	Q	E	E	Q	F	T	M	O	S
N	B	R	H	I	I	E	N	V	K	J	F	H	N	I	X	C	P
V	J	X	W	H	N	S	X	G	O	L	S	S	P	U	C	B	I
V	L	J	N	D	Z	H	X	I	I	F	R	E	B	S	X	C	J
A	Z	M	C	Q	S	U	I	A	K	G	N	V	R	E	J	U	I
A	C	I	M	R	S	Y	N	H	V	A	F	T	I	J	K	D	A
K	R	S	K	M	V	J	P	K	L	I	R	G	W	U	B	T	U
I	W	S	Y	K	Y	P	H	L	A	H	E	I	I	Q	Q	C	R
S	P	I	R	I	T	U	A	L	E	X	E	R	C	I	S	E	S
X	F	O	N	H	N	W	H	Q	Z	N	E	W	H	A	S	K	I
D	U	N	W	D	S	J	M	A	E	F	T	U	Y	G	U	N	F
C	J	A	M	Q	F	X	R	G	C	Y	T	F	K	L	C	Z	Y
P	S	R	H	T	E	B	A	Z	I	L	E	Y	X	L	G	K	L
L	T	Y	S	M	M	P	D	E	I	T	M	C	X	A	X	J	W

Note: Some words may appear backwards.

CHAPTER 25
Missions Abroad

Multiple Choice

Pick the best answer.

1. The Franciscans and Dominicans were the first missionaries to come over to the New World. Which nationality did they come with?

A. the Italians
B. the French
C. the Spanish
D. the Dutch

2. Missions were:

A. communities for the natives centered around the Church.
B. certain jobs, tasks, and goals the missionaries had.
C. the first churches built in the New World.
D. monasteries were missionaries lived.

3. How did the natives of Mexico respond to the Spanish efforts to evangelize them?

A. None converted and they grew violent toward the Spanish.
B. Some converted, but others continued their pagan ways, and some remained hostile to the Spanish.
C. All of them converted because of special miracles.
D. They wanted to live peacefully with the Spanish but did not want to convert to Christianity.

4. What saint is famous for ministering to African slaves?

A. Ignatius
B. Bartholome de las Casas
C. Rose of Lima
D. Peter Claver

5. What saint was a Third Order Dominican of African descent and labored among the poor and sick of Peru?

A. Ignatius
B. Bartholome de las Casas
C. Martin de Porres
D. Peter Claver

6. Who did Our Lady of Guadalupe appear to?

A. Juan Diego
B. Mother Mariana de Jesús Torres
C. Rose of Lima
D. Martin de Porres

7. In what country did Our Lady of Good Success appear?

A. Mexico
B. Ecuador
C. Peru
D. None of the above

8. Which of the following did the French missionaries *not* do?

A. spread the Gospel
B. establish the French fur trade
C. gather valuable geographical information about North America
D. squabble with Spanish missionaries about how to convert the natives

9. What nickname did the native tribes give the Jesuits?

A. Blackrobes
B. Blackcassocks
C. Blackhoods
D. Blackcapes

10. Which tribe killed the martyr Fr. Isaac Jogues?

A. Huron
B. Aztecs
C. Mohawk
D. Seminole

Writing Assignment: Converting a Native Tribe

Pretend you are a Jesuit priest who has just arrived at a native village. They don't know who you are and you don't speak their language. How would you go about the process of trying to convert them to Christianity? Make a list of 5–10 things you would try to accomplish or tell them about in your first six months there, and write a sentence or two of how you would go about doing each thing. Consider: How do you communicate with them? Which Christian teachings do you start with? How would you teach them those things?

CHAPTER 26
Jansenism and Gallicanism

Matching

Match each term with the statement or phrase that describes it.

A. Gallican liberties	D. *Unigenitus*	G. Gallicanism
B. Cornelius Jansen	E. Jansenism	H. *Augustinus*
C. Louis XIV	F. Henry of Navarre	

____ 1. certain privileges French bishops enjoyed that the bishops of other countries did not enjoy

____ 2. a heresy that said people couldn't keep all of God's commandments and Jesus did not die for all mankind, only a select few; appealed to intellectuals who thought it provided a superior form of Catholicism

____ 3. French king who helped put down several heresies

____ 4. a heresy that sought to block the pope's influence and power even on Church-related matters in a certain country's affairs

____ 5. book written by the heretic Cornelius Jansen

____ 6. founded the heresy of Jansenism

____ 7. Huguenot king who said "Paris is well worth a Mass" when he converted to Catholicism

____ 8. papal bull written by Pope Clement XI which condemned the Jansenism heresy

Double Puzzle

Unscramble the words below from chapter 26. Copy the letters in the numbered blocks to the blocks with the corresponding numbers at the bottom to help answer the question.

HOTSENUUG — 2

SENRIOCUL NEJSAN — 12, 7, 11

PEPO RUBNA — 9, 5

GKNI UOLIS — 3

JSNSANMEI — 8

HEYRN FO RAANREV — 10, 13, 4

LGSANLIMCAI — 1

SHNEEDALNRT — 6

A strange heretical movement originating in Paris that led to bizarre expressions of piety:

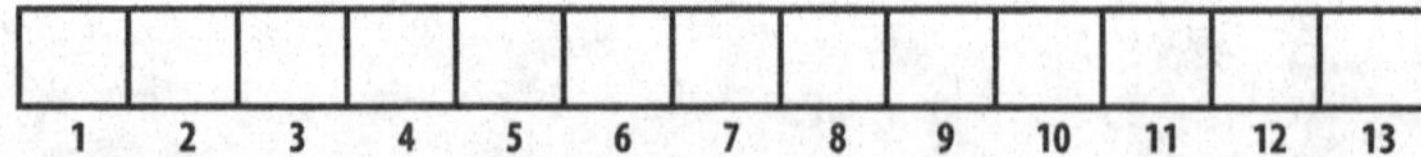

CHAPTER 27
The Age of Revolution

True or False?

In the blank beside each statement, write "T" if the statement is True or "F" if the statement is False. If the statement is False, change it to make it true. Either write a new statement in the margins or mark up the sentence itself.

____ 1. Anti-clericalism means opposition to religious authority or to the hierarchy of the Church.

____ 2. All Catholic leaders of Europe condemned the spirit of anti-clericalism.

____ 3. One aspect of anti-clericalism was making bishops swear an oath to the crown.

____ 4. The Enlightenment was a time of great religious and spiritual awakening across Europe.

____ 5. The order targeted the most by the spirit of anti-clericalism was the Dominicans.

____ 6. A radical group known as the Jacobins took over the French National Assembly, abolishing the monarchy and imprisoning the king and his family.

____ 7. Most of the people killed during the Reign of Terror were shot by firing squads.

____ 8. Napoleon Bonaparte led the Committee of Public Safety, the group responsible for the Reign of Terror.

Across

5. Catholic Holy Roman emperor who supported anti-clericalism
6. Device used to behead people
7. A time of scientific discovery
8. Order of priests who were victims of anti-clericalism
9. Opposition to religious authority

Down

1. Martyred during the French Revolution
2. Leader of the Committee of Public Safety
3. Successful French general
4. A time of great violence in France
8. Group that took over the French National Assembly

CHAPTER 28
After the Revolution

Fill in the Blank

Write an answer in the blank that best completes the statement.

1. Napoleon and Pope _____________ had a rocky relationship.
2. A _____________ is an agreement the Church enters into with the government of a nation.
3. Napoleon once held the pope as a _____________ in the northern Italian town of Savona.
4. A _____________ government means a government where people elect others to make laws.
5. The word *liberal* comes from the word _____________.
6. Pius VII called for the restoration of the _____________ in 1814 after years of being disbanded.
7. There was a brief Catholic reign in England under _____________.
8. The _____________ was an English law that repealed almost all of the old laws against Catholics and restored their political rights.
9. _____________ was a prominent Anglican clergyman and theologian who converted to Catholicism.
10. The first Catholic diocese in the United States was in _____________.

Word Search

Find the hidden words from chapter 28. For extra work, consider writing down something you read in the text about each person, place, or term you find.

Newman, Napoleon, Catholic Relief Act, Liberalism, Democratic, concordat, Pius, James

Note: Some words may appear backwards.

CHAPTER 29
The Age of Pius IX

Short Answer

Answer the following questions in a few complete sentences.

1. What actions did the Church take in the wake of the French Revolution and the spreading of liberal ideas?

2. How did Pope Pius IX respond when the Italian liberals tried to wrestle control of the Papal States away from him?

3. When the Italian king, Victor Emmanuel II, took control of the Papal States, why did Pius IX have the commander of the papal forces fire a few shots at the Italians before ultimately surrendering?

4. What sorts of actions did the anti-Catholic Italian state do to the Church?

5. What legacy did Pius IX leave behind? What sorts of things is he remember for?

Writing Assignment: Explaining the Immaculate Conception

In the space provided or on your computer, write 2–3 paragraphs explaining the Immaculate Conception. Pretend you are writing a letter to someone who doesn't understand this dogma or know what it is. What does it mean? Why is it important to Christians that Mary be conceived without sin? How does the Church justify this teaching if Jesus was sent to save all mankind, and Mary would not need saving if she never had sin on her soul? Do outside research if you must.

CHAPTER 30
A New Century With New Challenges

Multiple Choice

Pick the best answer.

1. Pope Pius IX was succeeded by:

A. Pius X.
B. Leo XIII.
C. Francis I.
D. Paul VI.

2. The word *communism* means:

A. living together on a commune.
B. the stealing of land.
C. eradicating poverty.
D. owning things in common.

3. An *atheist* is:

A. someone who does not believe God exists.
B. someone who champions Communism.
C. someone who doesn't believe in organized religion.
D. someone who often resorts to violence.

4. How did the popes of the time feel about Communism?

A. They liked that it sought to eradicate poverty.
B. They condemned it for many reasons.
C. They were indifferent to it.
D. They tried to say it was their idea.

5. What was Pope Leo's encyclical *Rerum Novarum* (*On the Condition of the Working Classes*) about?

A. the importance of peace
B. how to increase piety in one's daily life
C. social problems like poverty and working conditions
D. a restructuring of the hierarchy of the Church

6. What was the main error of Modernism?

A. They wanted to use technology to solve the world's problems.
B. They wanted to get rid of all old books.
C. They wanted to change parts of the Bible.
D. That thought that everything was subject to change, including God himself.

7. How did Pope St. Pius X take action against the Modernists?

A. He forbid them from teaching in seminaries and religious schools.
B. He discouraged Catholic publishers from publishing their writings and refused to promote Modernists to important Church offices.
C. He made all new priests swear an oath against Modernism.
D. All of the above.

8. Despite the errors of Communism, what country surprisingly was experiencing a Catholic renaissance in the late nineteenth century, led by figures like G. K. Chesterton and Hilaire Belloc?

A. Italy
B. Germany
C. England
D. Spain

9. Which of the following did *not* come out of the Third Council of Baltimore in 1884?

A. reforms made to the education of youth
B. a strategy for evangelizing Protestants
C. reforms to clerical discipline
D. the writing of The Baltimore Catechism

10 What did St. Thérèse of Lisieux call her way of living that stressed small acts of kindness and love?

A. The Little Way
B. The Small Way
C. The Loving Way
D. The Little Path

Writing Assignment: Living the Little Way

In the space provided, make a list of 10 things you can do in your daily life to live like St. Thérèse. What small acts of kindness can you do for those around you? What hidden ways can you draw closer to Jesus?

CHAPTER 31
Under Fascism and Communism

Matching

Match each term with the statement or phrase that describes it.

A. Miguel Pro
B. Jacinta
C. the Lateran Treaty
D. Francisco
E. public revelation
F. The Great War
G. Lucia
H. Cristeros
I. Benito Mussolini
J. Our Lady of Fatima
K. *Divini Redemptoris*
L. consecrate
M. private revelation
N. Fascists

____ 1. wanted a strong national government and leader who would suppress opposition and free speech; opposed Communism and democracy

____ 2. Jesuit Mexican priest martyred for the Faith

____ 3. Catholic militant group in Mexico that defended the Church against a corrupt socialist government

____ 4. encyclical that spoke out against Communism

____ 5. make something sacred by setting it apart for a specific religious cause

____ 6. those things revealed by God which all Catholics must believe

____ 7. raged from 1914 to 1918 and killed 16 million people

____ 8. visited three shepherd children in Portugal

____ 9. cousin to Francisco and Jacinta

____ 10. an agreement between the Church and the Italian government

____ 11. sister to Francisco

____ 12. fascist dictator of Italy

____ 13. divine messages given to an individual or group of individuals

____ 14. brother of Jacinta

Double Puzzle

Unscramble the words below from chapter 31. Copy the letters in the numbered blocks to the blocks with the corresponding numbers at the bottom to help answer the question.

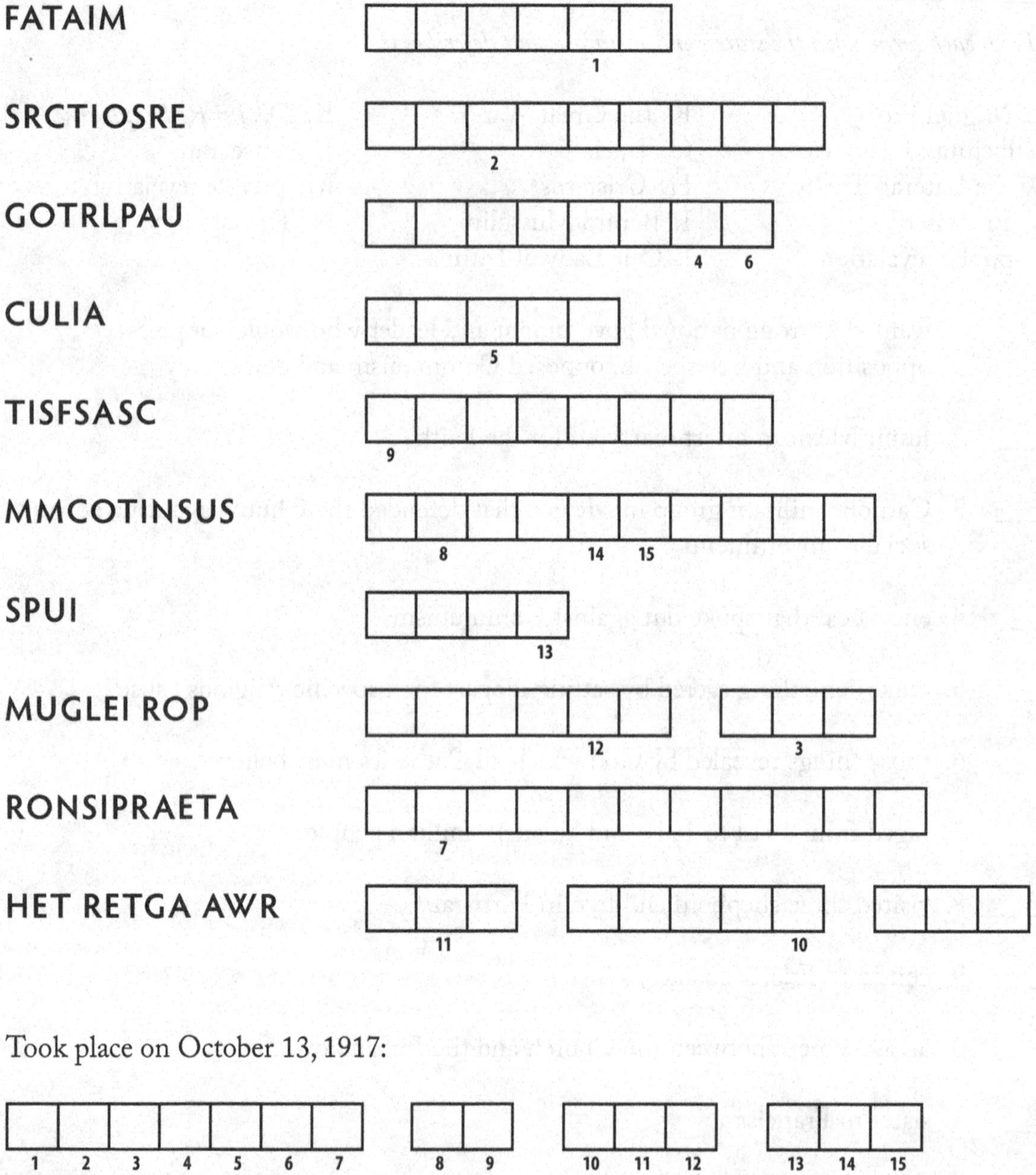

Took place on October 13, 1917:

1 2 3 4 5 6 7 8 9 10 11 12 13 14 15

CHAPTER 32
The Church in the Second World War

Fill in the Blank

Write an answer in the blank that best completes the statement.

1. The evil and violent German political party that provoked World War II was the ____________.

2. Hitler believed that the ____________ people were inferior to the German population and began to imprison and kill them.

3. Pope Pius XI wrote an ____________ condemning the Nazis.

4. The Nazis imprisoned Jews, Catholics, and others in ____________.

5. ____________ within Germany were faced with the difficult prospect of being suspected of treason to the German state for maintaining their loyalty to the Church.

6. ____________ gave up his own life to save a man with a family. He died at ____________.

7. ____________ hid and saved many Jewish people during the war, and was thus recognized as a hero among the Jewish people.

8. Hitler died by ____________.

Word Search

Find the hidden words from chapter 32. For extra work, consider writing down something you read in the text about each person, place, or term you find.

Hitler, Germany, Nazis, Kolbe, Pius, World War II, Auschwitz, concentration camp

C	R	Z	N	T	E	H	Z	C	P	I	R	H	F	G	J	I
S	O	H	H	B	Z	A	Y	T	J	T	H	E	J	C	F	F
S	P	N	L	E	H	Z	T	Z	E	N	V	Y	L	X	V	Q
T	B	O	C	Y	N	A	M	R	E	G	T	U	N	T	G	B
O	K	R	Y	E	Y	M	J	J	C	V	D	Z	X	W	I	S
O	T	Y	Y	K	N	C	N	A	R	S	A	U	T	O	W	H
W	J	W	I	I	M	T	U	J	R	I	V	R	B	R	A	B
P	S	C	S	Z	N	S	R	W	G	Z	L	J	W	L	W	A
Q	I	Z	I	B	C	G	S	A	T	A	C	T	V	D	Y	E
S	Q	S	O	H	S	L	Y	E	T	N	D	V	Z	W	S	Y
L	G	U	W	P	I	U	S	O	O	I	I	O	L	A	N	Q
C	M	I	R	W	U	Q	S	I	W	G	O	P	U	R	K	E
M	T	J	J	M	Z	R	D	G	T	K	Z	N	Q	I	E	Z
Z	D	C	K	K	R	G	R	O	G	K	U	T	C	I	L	V
V	F	V	Y	F	D	Y	Z	A	A	W	X	J	V	A	U	G
K	A	V	P	A	F	H	G	J	Q	Y	V	G	J	T	M	N
Y	F	T	J	E	M	D	U	L	K	R	N	K	J	K	O	P

Note: Some words may appear backwards.

CHAPTER 33
The Second Vatican Council

True or False?

In the blank beside each statement, write "T" if the statement is True or "F" if the statement is False. If the statement is False, change it to make it true. Either write a new statement in the margins or mark up the sentence itself.

____ 1. Mass attendance in Europe was high after World War II.

____ 2. After World War II, Catholicism struggled all over the world.

____ 3. The purpose of the Second Vatican Council was to change the Church's teachings.

____ 4. The Second Vatican Council took four years, from 1962 to 1965.

____ 5. Although Pope John XXIII summoned the council, he died before it was concluded.

____ 6. The *Novus Ordo Missae* was a new catechism put out by the Church as a result of the Second Vatican Council.

____ 7. The Novus Ordo threw Latin completely out of the Mass.

____ 8. The Second Vatican Council taught that Latin and Gregorian Chant should be preserved in the Novus Ordo.

Writing Assignment – Comparing and Contrasting the Old Rite and the Novus Ordo

In the space below, draw a line down the middle to make two columns (stop halfway down). Label one side "Old Rite" and the other "Novus Ordo." Make a list of how the two forms of the Mass are different. Then, underneath these lists, make a list of how the two are the same. Do outside research or talk to your parents if you need help.

CHAPTER 34
Hopes and Fears

Multiple Choice

Pick the best answer.

1. Ecumenism is:

A. when Catholics try to convert non-Catholic Christians.
B. when Catholics purposely avoid communication with non-Catholic Christians.
C. when Catholics work together with non-Catholic Christians.
D. when Catholics leave the Church for other Christian denominations.

2. What was it that helped bring a sense of unity between the Catholic Church and the Eastern Orthodox Church?

A. Both Churches suffered under Communism.
B. The two churches held a council where they worked out their differences.
C. The Orthodox Church took the blame for the schism in 1054.
D. Nothing, the two Churches still do not communicate with one another.

3. What controversial stance did Pope Paul VI take during his pontificate?

A. He met with leaders of the Eastern Orthodox Church.
B. He argued to remove Gregorian Chant from the Mass.
C. He told priests to celebrate Mass facing the congregation.
D. He wanted to take a lighter tone in the Church's opposition to Communism.

4. Dissent means:

A. when people start a secret "underground" Catholic Church.
B. when people break away from the Catholic Church to start their own.
C. when people disagree with the Church's Magisterium.
D. when people oust their parish priest.

5. Pope Paul VI's famous encyclical *Humanae Vitae* means:

A. On Human Life.
B. On Human Virtues.
C. On Human Feelings.
D. On Humanity and Virtue.

Crossword Puzzle

Across

2. Disagreeing with the Church's Magisterium
3. When Catholics work together with non-Catholic Christians
6. Acronym for the government-run Chinese church
8. Name for the "New Order of the Mass"
9. Communist country that tortured one of the Church's cardinals

Down

1. Pope Paul VI met with this other Christian faith
4. This spread throughout the Church after the Second Vatican Council
5. Wrote *Humanae Vitae*
7. Country where there was an underground Catholic Church

CHAPTER 35
The Pontificate of Pope St. John Paul II

Fill in the Blank

Write an answer in the blank that best completes the statement.

1. Pope ______________ died after only thirty-three days on the throne.

2. Karol Wojtyla, who took the name John Paul II upon being elected pope, was from the country of ______________.

3. Karol Wojtyla was the first ______________ to be elected to the papacy since 1522.

4. A Turkish assassin shot John Paul II on______________, the same date as the first apparition of Our Lady of Fatima.

5. John Paul II published a new ______________ to serve as a reference for people who wanted to learn about the Church.

6. John Paul II sought new and fresh ways to teach the Catholic faith. He named his efforts to do this the ______________.

Double Puzzle

Unscramble the words below from chapter 35. Copy the letters in the numbered blocks to the blocks with the corresponding numbers at the bottom to help answer the question.

JNOH LPAU

EVCOCANL

WEN IONEAZALNEIVGT

MUNCOMMIS

SAINSSSA

TIESCCAHM

IONR RUCNITA

WRWAAS

CAALINRD

At John Paul II's famous Mass in Poland, the people chanted this.

__ __ (1 2) __ __ __ __ (3 4 5 6) __ __ __ (7 8 9) !

CHAPTER 36
The Church in the Twenty-First Century

Writing Assignment: Looking Back

Answer the following question in a few paragraphs, either in the space provided or on your computer.

What was your favorite aspect of the Church history you learned in this book? Which part interested you the most? What stories, characters, and moments grabbed your attention? Explain why.

Writing Assignment: Looking Ahead

Answer the following question in a few paragraphs, either in the space provided or on your computer.

Knowing what you know about Church history and where the Church stands today, what do you think the Church needs to do to flourish in the next fifty years? How can the Church better evangelize around the world and convert people who live in a secular culture that forgets or even attacks God? How can the Church help fix the modern world's problems and lead people to heaven?

ANSWER KEY

CHAPTER 1
Christ and the Apostles

Short Answer

1. The apostles were gathered in the Upper Room in Jerusalem, along with Mary and many of Jesus's other disciples when the Holy Spirit descended upon them, appearing as tongues of fire. They had been gathered for nine days of prayer following Christ's ascension. When the Spirit filled them, they were able to go out and preach to the thousands gathered in the street, speaking in several different languages. This amazed the people and many were baptized that very day. This is seen as the birth of the Church because this was when the apostles began their mission of spreading the Church and fulfilling the call Jesus gave them to "go out and make disciples of all nations."

2. Apostle means "one who is sent."
   Answers will vary for second part.

3. With the Tower of Babel, mankind sought to build a tower to reach the heavens but did so through their pride. As a result, God scattered them into many tribes, and suddenly, they were each speaking different tongues. At Pentecost, the apostles, filled with the Holy Spirit, were able to speak different languages and in that way, bring the people back together to form the Church, the true "tower" that leads to heaven.

4. The apostles ordained men known as presbyters—sometimes called "elders" in the Bible—to help them in their sacramental ministry. These presbyters would become the first priests. With apostles (the first bishops), along with their presbyters and deacons, we see the basic structure of the Catholic Church's hierarchy.

5. Original name was Saul
   • Once persecuted Christians until his conversion, which took place after Christ appeared to him on the road to Damascus
   • Paul was a Jew, but preached mainly to Gentiles, non-Jews, which is why he came to be seen as the "Apostle of the Gentiles."
   • Wrote many letters which were included in the New Testament
   • Suffered a martyr's death
   • See text for more…

Crossword Puzzle

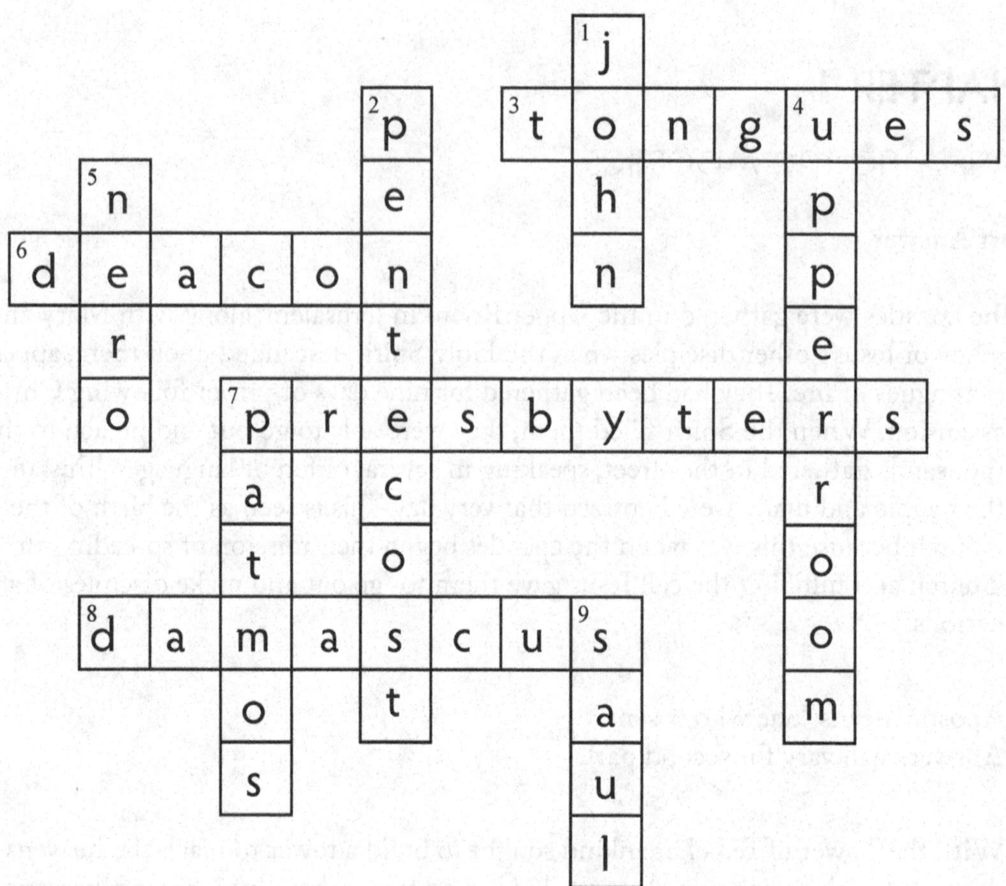

CHAPTER 2

The Apostolic Age

Multiple Choice

Pick the best answer.

1. A
2. B
3. B
4. D
5. C

Word Search

N	Q	M	A	Z	M	H	W	U	B	T	V	X	K	S
P	O	S	U	I	T	A	N	G	I	R	E	N	T	P
X	R	I	S	E	H	I	B	M	O	A	B	O	H	O
A	P	A	K	K	V	A	L	U	K	D	Q	X	E	H
G	P	U	C	E	F	D	P	F	G	I	S	Z	S	S
H	L	O	R	Y	A	T	L	R	H	T	E	X	S	I
U	B	S	S	L	L	T	Q	X	V	I	X	M	A	B
Z	A	I	P	T	H	O	P	I	F	O	U	C	L	E
L	P	V	N	Q	O	A	P	L	E	N	F	Y	O	U
J	Y	V	C	V	N	L	M	E	O	P	Q	Y	N	H
L	E	K	X	M	O	J	I	I	U	B	P	J	I	S
H	O	M	K	W	I	D	Y	C	U	A	W	Q	A	P
I	T	T	K	G	N	J	A	G	A	K	S	E	N	R
U	O	P	R	O	G	X	Y	D	H	G	O	W	S	B
O	S	Z	A	P	D	I	D	U	C	G	E	J	N	E

CHAPTER 3
The Apologists

Answers will vary.

CHAPTER 4
Roman Persecutions

Matching

1. B
2. G
3. F
4. A
5. E
6. H
7. C
8. D

Writing Assignment: Short Story

Stories will vary.

CHAPTER 5
Dissent and Heresy

Multiple Choice

1. C
2. B
3. D
4. B
5. A

Double Puzzle

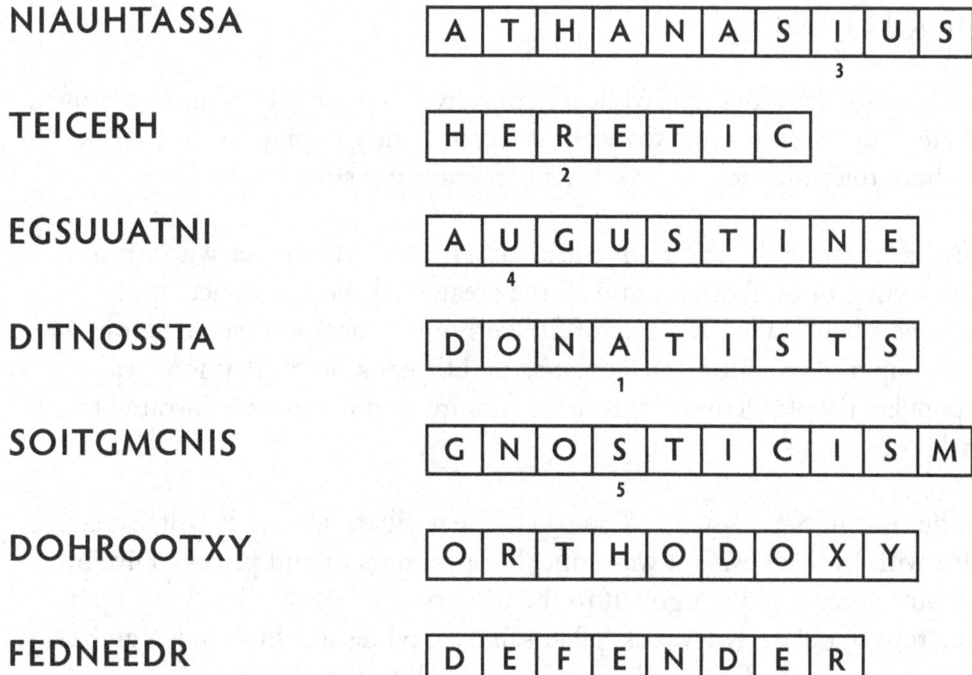

The Arian heresy was named after this man:

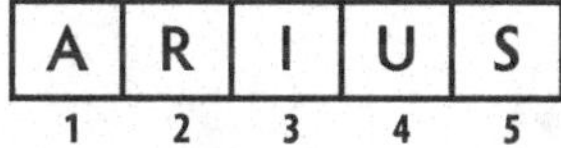

CHAPTER 6

Christian Monasticism

Short Answer

Answer the following questions in a few complete sentences.

1.

- He lived during the third and fourth centuries.
- Lived in Egypt in the city of Thebes, but after being turned over to the Roman authorities, he fled into the desert to hide. There he took refuge in a cave.
- He decided to stay in that cave and focus on praying and growing closer to God. He lived there for about one year!
- He prayed, fasted, and became a friend of God.
- When his clothes rotted away, he used the leaves of the palm trees to cover himself, and his beard grew long and wild. He drank from the spring, ate the fruit of the palm trees, and was occasionally brought food by the birds.

- He is known as the first Christian hermit and Desert Father.

2. St. Anthony of the Desert

3. Monks, like hermits, live alone, but while a hermit lives completely on his or her own, monks live alone in cells but come together as a community to pray, eat, and work. Monks also have rules that govern how their community is structured.

4. St. Anthony had a young disciple from Alexandria named Athanasius who wrote down all the sayings of St. Anthony and all the great deeds he had done. These writings became a book called The Life of St. Anthony. Athanasius would go on to become bishop of Alexandria and a great saint. His book on St. Anthony was extremely popular. People all over the Roman Empire read it and were inspired to live like St. Anthony.

5. A group of hermits in Syria who lived on top of great pillars. Unlike Egypt, Syria was crowded with large cities, so it was difficult for hermits to find places to live by themselves. Since they could not go out to the wilderness, these Stylites went up by living on the tops of pillars. Known as "pillar saints," Stylites like St. Simeon and St. Daniel spent years on top of pillars that could be as tall as sixty feet.

Crossword Puzzle

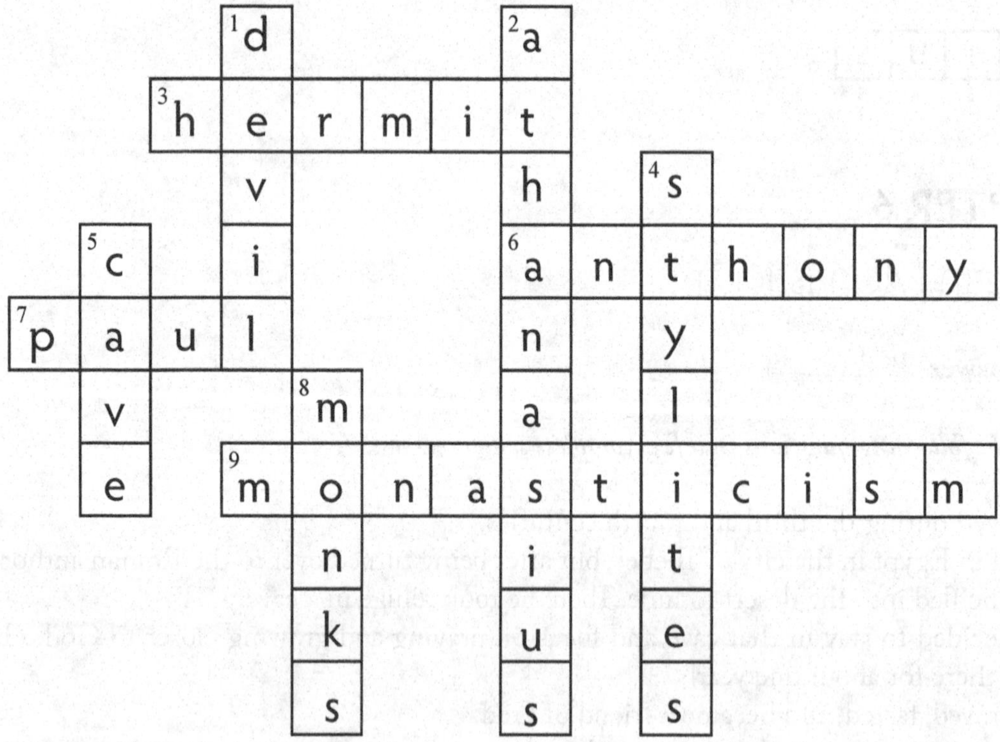

CHAPTER 7
The Triumph of the Church

Matching

1. D
2. F
3. H
4. B
5. I
6. E
7. A
8. J
9. G
10. C

Writing Assignment: Make a List

Answers will vary.

CHAPTER 8
The Benedictines

True or False?

1. F, The empire still had political problems—it was split in two—and barbarians invaded their lands.
2. F, St. Benedict should be replaced by St. Augustine.
3. T
4. T
5. F, He came from a noble family who sent him to school.
6. T
7. T
8. F, It means "prayer and work."
9. T
10. F, Some tried to poison him.

Writing Assignment: Write Your Own "Rule"

Answers will vary.

CHAPTER 9

A Time of Missionaries

Multiple Choice

Pick the best answer.

1. B
2. C
3. D
4. C
5. A

Writing Assignment: Converting the Nations

Armenia:
Converted to the Christian faith under the influence of the great miracle worker St. Gregory Thaumaturgus (d. 270). To this day, Armenia holds the distinction of being the first Christian nation.

Ireland:
The conversion of this once-pagan nation is mostly attributed to St. Patrick. After being kidnapped by pirates and sold into slavery, he was held captive by the Druids for several years. But Patrick was able to escape and made his way to Rome. Soon thereafter, he was ordained a bishop and returned to Ireland to convert the people who had formerly been his captors. For the next several decades, St. Patrick went about Ireland converting people to the Catholic faith and founding monasteries. Others would continue his holy work, such as St. Brigid of Kildare, who founded the first convent in Ireland. St. Enda founded a monastic school on the island of Aran that formed other Irish monks as missionaries. For three centuries, Irish missionaries tromped about the European continent establishing monasteries and preaching Christ.

France:
Once ruled by the pagan Franks, the nation that would become France came to be known as the "Eldest Daughter of the Church" because it was the first pagan kingdom within the boundaries of the old Roman Empire to embrace the Catholic faith. This happened because Clovis married a Christian princess named Clotilde. At first, Clovis resisted Christianity, especially after one of his children was baptized and died shortly thereafter. But once, while engaged in a heated battle, Clovis cried out to the Christian God for help and won. He attributed his victory to this and began to convert the rest of his kingdom.

Spain:
The peninsula of Spain was once overrun by a barbarian tribe called the Visigoths, who eventually embraced the Arian heresy. But they were slowly won over to the Catholic faith by the preaching of two saintly brothers, St. Isidore of Seville and St. Leander. In 587, the Visigothic king Reccared I renounced Arianism and embraced Catholic Christianity. Most Visgothic nobles followed his example. Zealous bishops held local councils reforming the life of the clergy and laity throughout Spain. For the next century and a half, Visigothic Spanish culture would flourish under the government of pious Catholic kings and disciplined clergy.

England:
Pope St. Gregory the Great had a desire to convert the Anglo-Saxons living on the island of Britain, so he sent a Benedictine monk named Augustine and a few companions there to preach the Catholic faith. In 597, Augustine met with the pagan king Ethelbert. Though the king did not immediately convert, he allowed Augustine to preach freely and gave him some land at Canterbury to build a church. Augustine set up the first English diocese at Canterbury; today, he is remembered as St. Augustine of Canterbury. Ethelbert would eventually convert, along with his wife, Bertha, who became Saint Bertha of Kent. Many Anglo-Saxons accepted Christianity and some violence ensued between those who remained pagan, but Christianity gradually spread, so that within a century, almost all of England was Christian.

CHAPTER 10

Rome and the Byzantines

Matching

1. B
2. A
3. E
4. C
5. F
6. G
7. D

Word Search

E	A	H	G	A	C	M	E	G	G	P	A	T	D	B
H	X	V	C	F	A	B	E	V	R	V	A	G	X	V
J	J	C	F	H	H	W	E	Y	E	S	R	T	N	N
A	E	T	O	R	U	L	C	C	G	P	H	J	D	U
M	A	V	J	M	N	S	I	J	O	I	A	L	E	D
L	Q	C	B	T	M	E	N	P	R	Y	L	X	E	E
H	J	T	S	W	C	U	E	H	I	G	L	I	X	Q
C	L	W	M	Y	W	G	N	D	A	Z	A	M	Y	F
E	T	U	W	A	R	N	W	I	N	C	C	R	I	P
L	L	R	M	E	L	B	B	X	C	B	Y	A	P	L
L	T	V	G	T	C	S	I	S	H	A	J	O	I	Y
N	X	O	Z	V	D	E	I	X	A	F	T	Y	C	L
E	R	T	B	V	G	Y	N	L	N	T	O	E	J	C
Y	P	D	T	U	Y	C	F	T	T	M	K	R	D	N
O	E	L	R	O	R	E	P	M	E	I	C	O	N	W

CHAPTER 11
The Carolingians

Short Answer

1. Martel was the mayor of the palace to the Frankish (French) king, but he wielded more power than his title granted because the king was weak. As the Muslim armies took over Spain and moved to invade France, Martel led a host of Frankish warriors and marched to a place called Tours where he defeated the Moorish threat. If he had not been victorious at Tours, the Muslim armies would have conquered France and swept into western Europe.

2. Like his father, Pepin was second in command but actually wielded much of the power in the kingdom. This frustrated him. He got Pope Zachary II to admit the person who truly controlled the kingdom should actually be ruler. Zachery issued a papal bull confirming this, giving Pepin the justification he needed to overthrow the Merovingians. He captured the last Merovingian king, Childeric III, and cut his hair off—a symbol of his royal authority—before sending him to a monastery. Pepin proclaimed himself king of the Franks in 751.

3. Pepin did not forget how the pope had helped him, and soon the popes would need his help in return when they were harassed by the Lombards, a powerful tribe who had set up a kingdom in northern Italy. Pepin marched into Italy and defeated the Lombards, giving much of the land in central Italy to the papacy to be the Church's own territory. Pepin thought that if the popes had their own territory, they would have more security and not be as prone to threats from other kingdoms. These lands were called the Papal States.

4.
   - Charles was the son of Pepin. His people called him Charlemagne, which means "Charles the Great." He was an energetic and brave ruler and is considered the greatest ruler the Franks ever had.
   - He won many battles, including the conquering of Germany, where he compelled the pagan tribes there to accept Christianity. He also beat back barbarian invaders from the east and extended Frankish power into Italy to protect the pope. He ruled most of western Europe.
   - He was also a very pious man. He had a chapel built in his palace, surrounded himself with monks, built monasteries, befriended popes, and made sure the clergy in his realm were well-educated. At one point, he saved Pope Leo III from a massive riot in Rome.
   - One Christmas in Rome, in the year 800, while Charlemagne was praying at Mass, Pope Leo approached him and placed a crown on his head. He declared Charlemagne to be Roman emperor. From the year 800 onward, Charlemagne went by the title

emperor. In crowning Charlemagne, the pope taught that the imperial power had passed from Byzantium to the Franks.
- Charlemagne died in 814, but his descendants retained control of his kingdom until the year 987.

5. One of the famous missionaries of the Carolingian era was St. Boniface. Boniface was sent by the pope to preach to various pagan tribes living in central and northern Germany. In one of his first encounters with a tribe called the Hessians, Boniface was told that they were accustomed to making sacrifices to the gods at a great oak tree. In bold defiance of their gods, St. Boniface chopped the oak tree down and taught the Hessians to honor Jesus Christ instead. He went on to build churches and became their bishop.

Crossword Puzzle

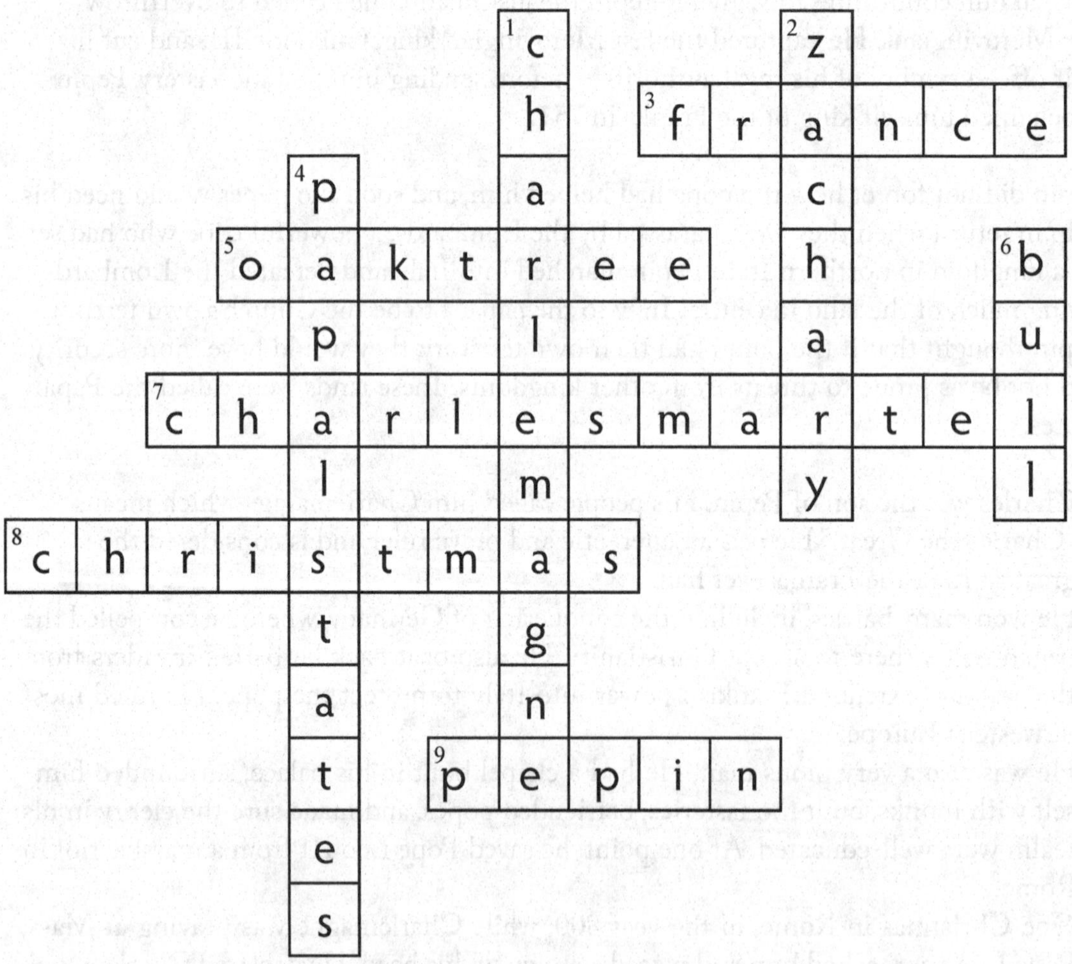

CHAPTER 12

Dark Days for the Papacy

True or False?

1. T
2. F; He put Formosus on trial *after* he had died!
3. T
4. F; He was originally from Germany.
5. F; He regretted doing this because Otto controlled much of the Church and sought to undermine his authority.
6. F; An *antipope* is a man who claims to be pope but is in fact not the real pope.
7. T
8. T

Double Puzzle

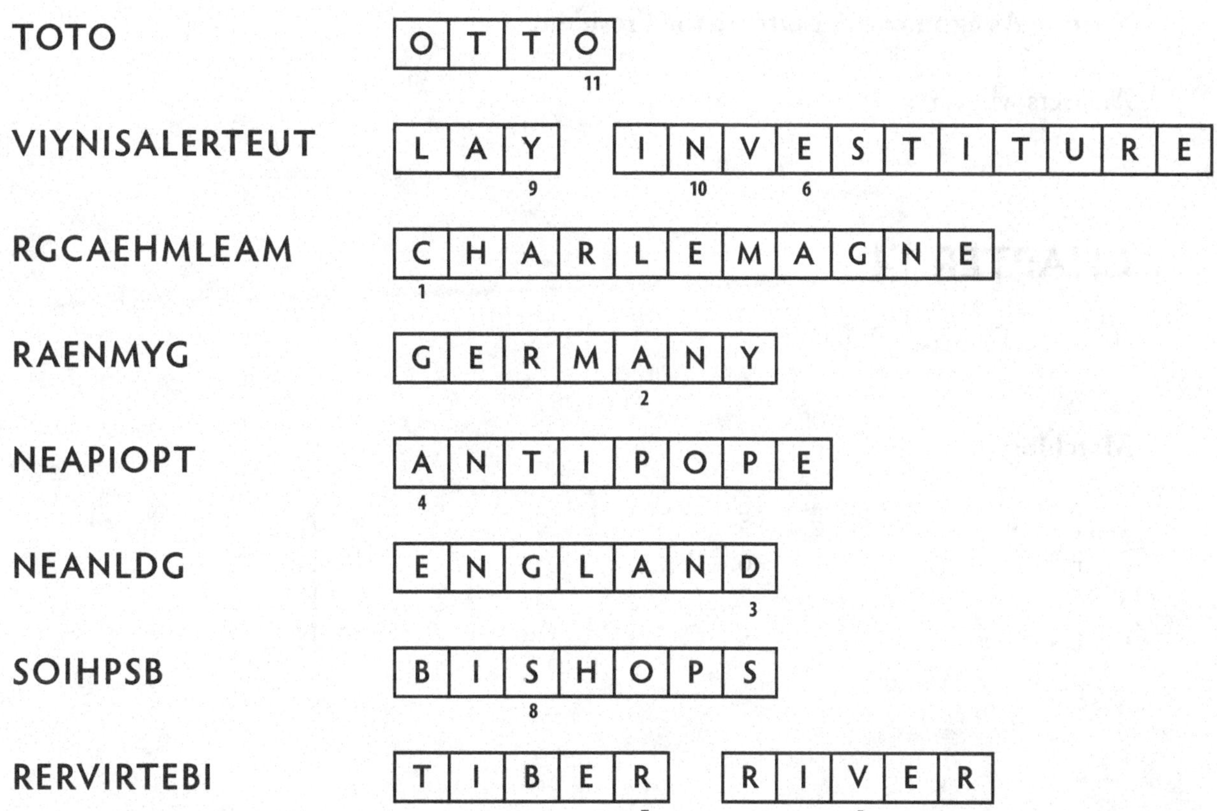

The name given to the trial where one pope put a deceased pope on trial.

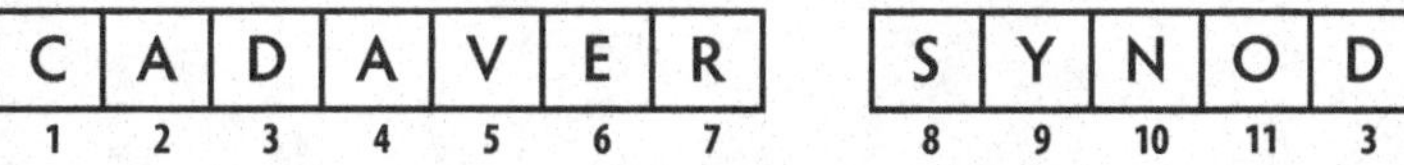

CHAPTER 13
The Struggle Against Lay Authority

Multiple Choice

Pick the best answer.

1. B
2. C
3. D
4. C
5. A
6. B
7. A
8. D

Writing Assignment: A Letter to the President

Answers will vary.

CHAPTER 14
The Crusading Ideal

Matching

1. E	5. G	9. A
2. F	6. B	10. I
3. D	7. J	11. K
4. L	8. C	12. H

Word Search

E	I	N	Y	A	G	W	S	C	T	C	H	E	F	X
M	C	T	E	N	J	R	C	U	K	O	J	N	G	J
E	R	N	C	W	A	Q	R	M	S	N	G	I	A	S
B	P	M	E	L	Q	K	I	P	N	S	B	T	H	V
E	G	E	P	G	S	B	I	I	K	T	Q	N	S	Y
V	R	M	N	T	L	T	E	K	B	A	H	A	C	R
C	E	W	M	A	A	U	G	V	P	N	Z	Z	H	C
T	P	J	I	L	N	F	D	D	R	T	H	Y	I	C
G	B	C	L	Y	C	C	M	N	A	I	T	B	S	G
P	F	E	W	D	K	T	E	V	I	N	U	B	M	A
H	R	C	R	U	S	A	D	E	U	O	G	H	I	K
S	I	L	Z	F	B	G	Y	O	N	P	L	R	T	H
N	O	B	S	L	N	I	Q	S	T	L	P	G	W	R
B	H	T	I	H	H	R	M	H	U	E	E	J	Y	F
A	I	H	P	O	S	A	I	G	A	H	C	C	G	V

CHAPTER 15

Monastic Reform Movements

True or False?

1. T
2. F; Norbert actually had great wealth resulting from his work for the emperor, until one day a near death experience caused him to rethink his life.
3. F; They used a version written by St. Augustine of Hippo.
4. F; It's a monastery in which monks and nuns live together under the same roof, though in two separate wings.
5. T
6. T
7. F; He founded many Cistercian monasteries.
8. T
9. T
10. F; She was the queen of Hungary.

Crossword Puzzle

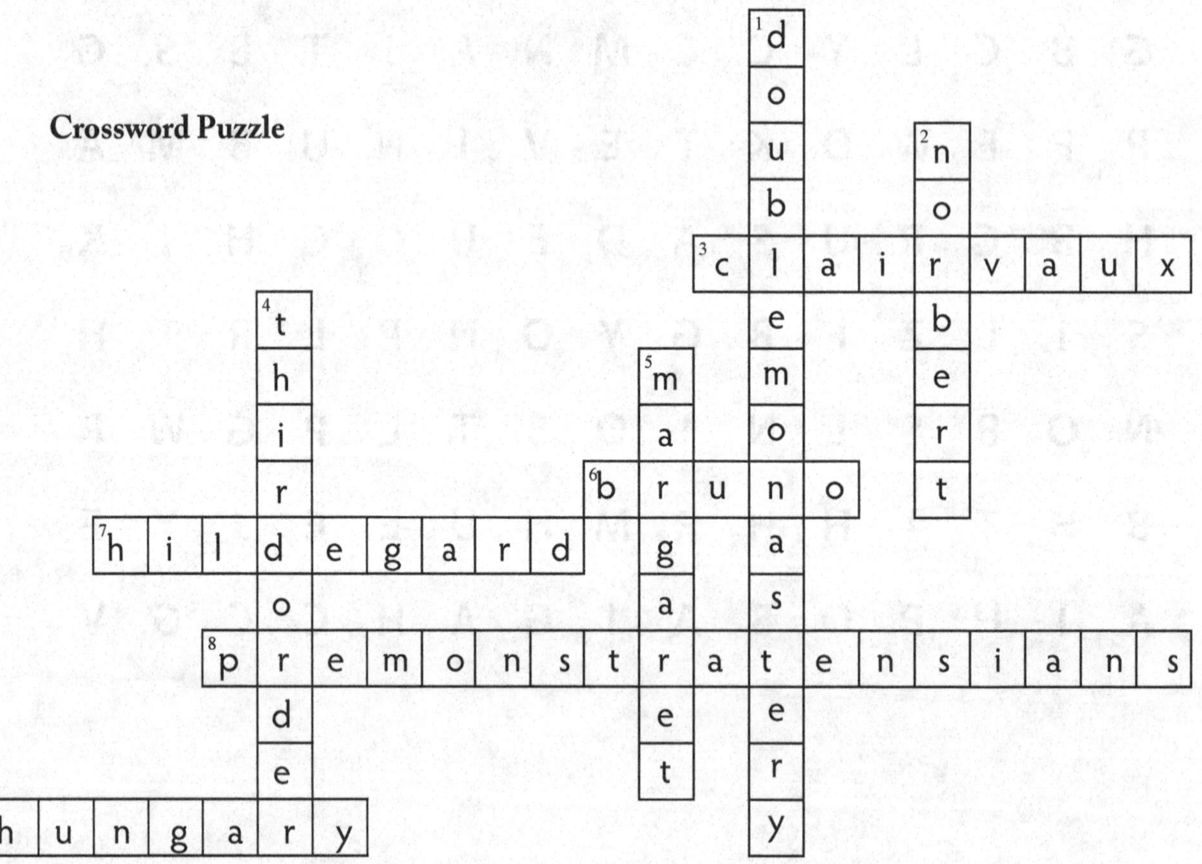

CHAPTER 16

The Mendicant Orders

1. • Bishops could still get wrapped up in worldly and political problems.
   • Powerful kings still tried to manipulate the Church.
   • In some places, the education and spiritual formation of priests was poor.
   • There was a sense among the people that the Church was not attending to the spiritual needs of average Christians.
   • Wandering preachers were beginning to spread dangerous heresies.

2. Francis di Bernadone was his given name. He was the son of a wealthy cloth merchant of Assisi, Italy. Young Francis lived a carefree life of feasting, drinking, and having parties with his friends. But more than anything, Francis wanted to be a knight and do brave deeds in battle. But his visions of glory did not go as planned as Assisi lost the battle and he spent time as a prisoner. A pilgrimage to Rome changed his life and led him to living a life of poverty.

3. While Francis was praying in the chapel, the crucifix above the altar began to speak to him, saying, "Go and rebuild my Church which, as you can see, is crumbling."

   Francis thought our Lord meant to rebuild San Damiano, so he went about gathering stones to restore the ruined chapel. But soon Francis realized that our Lord meant for Francis to rebuild the Church not with stone but by his example. Francis's devotion to poverty and simplicity would be the medicine to counteract the worldliness of the Church in his age.

4. *Mendicant* comes from a Latin word for begging, and a mendicant order is a religious order that survives from begging. This describes what Francis and his followers did.

5. At first, some people were unsure about Francis. It was uncommon for people to voluntarily live in poverty at that time and some were suspicious of him; some even suspected he was leading people into heresy with new and strange teachings. Francis went to Rome to meet Pope Innocent III to ask him to approve his way of life. At first, Pope Innocent thought Francis's idea of living in absolute poverty was not practical. He sent Francis away without approving his order. But according to legend, after sending Francis away, the pope had a dream that changed everything. He dreamed he saw a mighty church teetering and about to fall over, but then a man in a little brown habit came and held the church up, preventing its collapse. Innocent recognized the man in the dream as Francis. Francis again had an audience with the pope and Innocent approved Francis's way of life in 1209.

Writing Assignment: Why the Rosary is so important

Answers will vary.

CHAPTER 17
Scholasticism

Multiple Choice

Pick the best answer.

1. B
2. C
3. D
4. D
5. A
6. B
7. C
8. A
9. B
10. C

Double Puzzle

QUNSAIA

A Q U I N A S
14 16 5

TEARIOTLS

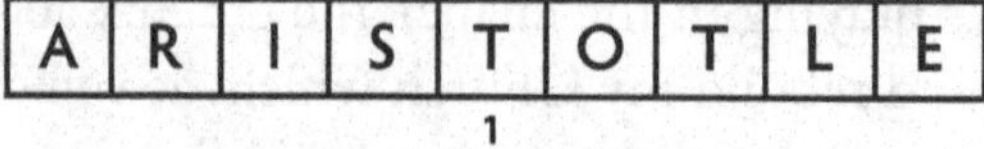

RTHECRA

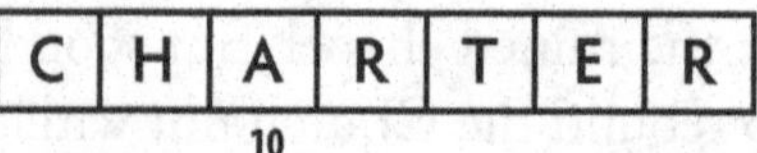

VURNYIIEST

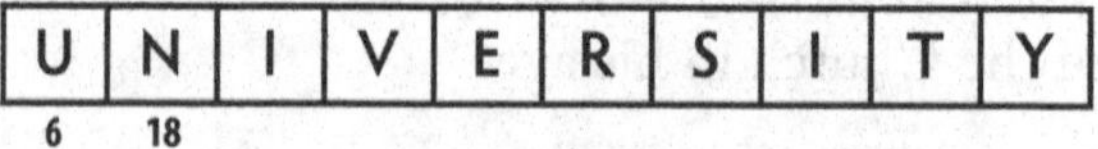

POPLYHHOSI

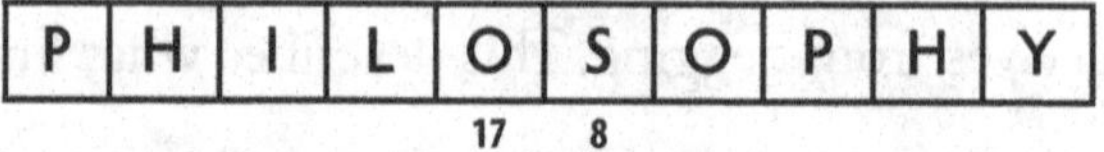

HYOLOGTE

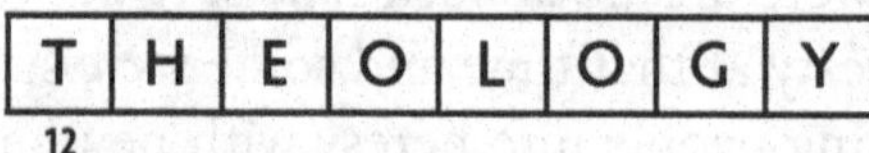

SAMMU

S U M M A
3

TIISSCMSOCHAL

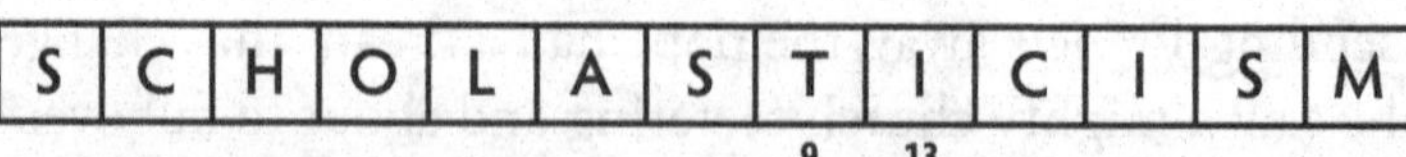

TESMONRAY

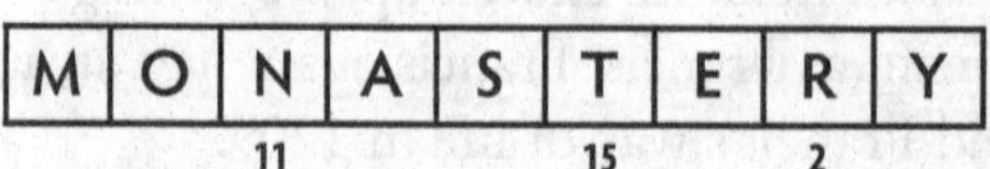

BNRUENETVAU

B O N A V E N T U R E
7 4

The theological word the Church uses to describe how the bread and wine of the Eucharist turn into the Body and Blood of Christ at Mass.

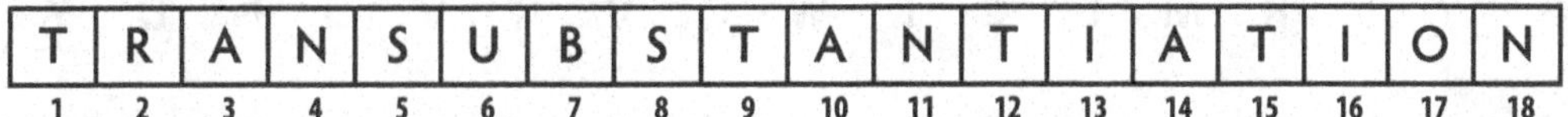

T	R	A	N	S	U	B	S	T	A	N	T	I	A	T	I	O	N
1	2	3	4	5	6	7	8	9	10	11	12	13	14	15	16	17	18

CHAPTER 18

Kings Versus Popes

Matching

1. H
2. G
3. K
4. J
5. D
6. C
7. F
8. E
9. B
10. A
11. I

Writing Assignment: Church and State

Answers will vary.

CHAPTER 19

The Babylonian Captivity

True or False?

1. F; They were afraid of him but he worked behind the scenes to get a Frenchman elected.
2. T
3. F; Rome was a filthy, violent, and hot place to live and he didn't like it. He moved the papal court to Avignon, France.
4. F; Most did not like it and thought the pope would become a puppet of the French king.
5. T
6. T
7. T
8. F; They featured two characters engaged in combat.
9. T
10. T

Word Search

J	H	G	W	L	R	M	F	C	K	W	Q	V	R	V	O	N	D	Y
X	B	F	F	K	I	R	L	C	E	A	V	D	W	V	A	U	T	M
T	O	F	V	W	L	E	B	T	W	E	P	C	H	X	X	I	D	M
L	N	D	Z	Q	M	G	W	N	G	E	L	C	N	K	V	Z	F	L
Z	I	C	H	E	Z	I	M	B	G	B	D	Z	H	I	Z	I	U	A
O	F	M	N	R	G	L	Q	J	C	F	Q	Q	T	R	O	G	W	A
R	A	T	N	O	N	G	I	V	A	Y	F	P	C	O	F	P	G	E
F	C	J	Z	H	I	V	O	E	Z	S	A	H	G	L	Z	N	E	M
U	E	K	Q	R	O	K	D	Z	V	C	R	L	T	L	L	F	W	S
T	E	Y	F	P	Z	M	R	W	N	E	H	E	P	Q	O	B	P	A
G	G	P	U	A	U	M	Y	A	L	C	R	Y	M	O	X	J	I	N
Y	W	L	R	H	J	M	I	E	I	U	T	Y	E	M	L	R	L	V
V	T	A	D	G	W	N	S	G	N	L	F	E	M	W	U	K	I	N
D	O	Y	K	F	O	K	H	U	W	C	J	N	Y	A	H	M	H	U
I	P	L	E	L	X	X	L	P	O	K	U	K	U	Y	N	W	P	H
E	Z	N	Y	C	A	T	H	E	R	I	N	E	K	T	T	Z	A	I
C	V	B	E	H	H	H	T	L	D	B	V	I	K	V	B	O	M	N
K	A	P	G	O	I	U	F	P	X	I	W	B	L	Y	J	N	F	N
B	N	W	I	A	R	V	H	R	J	A	G	N	U	U	X	C	W	Q

CHAPTER 20
The Great Western Schism

Short Answer

Answer the following questions in a few complete sentences.

1. After so many years with only French popes, the Italians rioted in the streets demanding an Italian pope. This led to the election of Urban VI, a quick tempered man who many did not like, including the French, who began to plot against him.

2. This was the time period where two men claimed to be pope. The French were unhappy about the election of Pope Urban VI and began plotting against him. A group of them met without Urban and issued a declaration that Urban's election was invalid. They claimed that they only elected him because they were afraid of the mob and that there was no pope. Then, led by the French cardinals, they elected the archbishop of Cambrai, Robert of Geneva, who took the name Clement VII. Clement and his supporters promptly moved back to Avignon and excommunicated Urban. Urban, meanwhile, claimed Clement was an antipope and took drastic measures against him, including raising money to prepare for a war. Different bands of Christians each supported a different pope. Thus, it was a time of great confusion for the Church.

3. It was a very confusing time for the Church because the people did not know who the real pope was and they did not know who to listen to. If a decree was issued, the people would not know if it was valid. Further, each pope nominated their own cardinals, bishops, and priests, meaning it was unclear if these men were actual clergymen. The Schism caused much confusion and even led to violence, as well as political posturing. If it benefited a certain kingdom to support a certain pope, they would. Multiple efforts to end the Schism failed because the popes refused to resign from office.

4. This council was called to try to put an end to the Great Western Schism. The Council of Pisa declared both the Roman and Avignon popes deposed; *deposed* means removed from their position. With both other popes gone, the Council of Pisa elected a new pope. But there was no precedent in Church history or theology to support the idea that cardinals could get rid of a sitting pope. Thus, the two other popes did not recognize the Council of Pisa and refused to step down. This meant there were now *three* men claiming to be pope! The third pope set up his court at Pisa, making the situation even worse.

5. Most historians and theologians teach that the popes at Rome were always the real popes. All the other claimants are considered antipopes, though the Church has never made an authoritative pronouncement on the question.

Writing Assignment – The Importance of the Church's Unity

Answers will vary.

CHAPTER 21

Late Medieval Mysticism

Multiple Choice

1. D
2. B
3. C
4. A
5. B
6. C
7. B
8. A

Crossword Puzzle

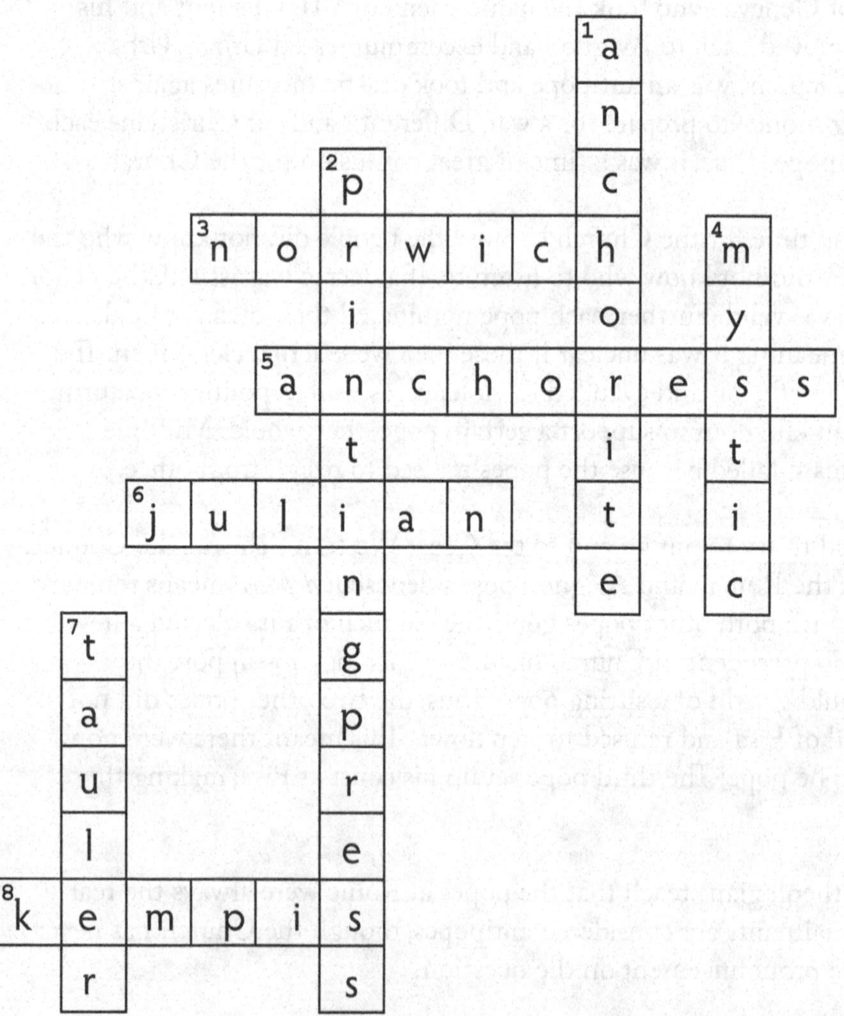

CHAPTER 22
The Outbreak of Protestantism

Matching

1. E
2. G
3. P
4. A
5. L
6. I
7. B
8. N
9. C
10. J
11. O
12. K
13. F
14. H
15. M
16. D

Writing Assignment – Characters of the Reformation

Martin Luther
Was a German Augustinian friar who had been troubled by simony and other scandals in his diocese relating to the sale of indulgences. This prompted Luther to write a document known as the *95 Theses*, which he posted on the door of the cathedral at Wittenberg in October of 1517. The *95 Theses* were a series of statements that called into question the Church's teachings on indulgences, purgatory, and the authority of the pope. Luther denied the authority of the Church's councils and taught that the Bible alone was the only authority a Christian needed. He also believed that people did not need to do penance for their sins. He taught faith alone—without anything else—was all one needed to be saved. Pope Leo X excommunicated Luther in 1520, but many princes and knights in Germany supported Luther. They hoped to use his movement to break Germany away from the Catholic Church and use his movement as an excuse to seize the Church's lands. Aided by powerful nobles, city after city throughout Germany fell under Luther's heresy. In places where his teachings took hold, Church property was seized and handed over to the government authorities. All over Germany, preachers were installed who would preach Luther's teachings, which had become known as Lutheranism.

John Calvin
Calvin was a French lawyer who shot to fame by writing a book called *Institutes of the Christian Religion*. The *Institutes* proposed a whole new understanding of Christianity different from Luther or the Catholic Church. The most well-known of his beliefs was the teaching of *predestination*, which states that God decides from all eternity who will go to heaven and who will go to hell. This teaching is very different from the Catholic view, which teaches that our actions have real consequences. Calvin also taught that Jesus Christ did not die for all men, only for the righteous, and that there should be no bishops. He wanted the church to have no real authority above the parish level. He thought parishes should be

ruled by groups of elders—called presbyters—who would select a pastor. Calvin's book and his teachings became very influential throughout France. Those Frenchmen who followed Calvin's teachings were known as Huguenots, and for a time there was violence between them and the Catholics as they battled for the throne.

King Henry VIII

King Henry VIII ruled England from 1509 to 1547. At first, he was a big opponent of Martin Luther and the other reformers who opposed the Catholic Church. He had even been granted the title "Defender of the Faith" by the pope. But by 1527, Henry's wife, Catherine of Aragon, had been unable to produce a son and heir for the king. Henry began to lose interest in Catherine and became enamored with Anne Boleyn, a noblewoman of the court. He tried to get his marriage annulled but Pope Clement VII refused. This made Henry so angry he began to threaten the pope. Meanwhile, Anne Boleyn was sympathetic to Martin Luther. As Henry moved closer to Anne—and as he got angrier with the Church—he considered the advantages that might come from breaking with Rome. Eventually, Henry decided that he wanted to be in control of the Church in England. He passed a law forcing every cleric and royal official to swear an oath that he was the Supreme Head of the Church in England. Once he did this, he sent Catherine away and married Anne instead. He replaced Catholic bishops with men loyal to him and had the Catholic Mass thrown out and replaced with a service that was much more in line with what Luther had envisioned. This new Church Henry created is called the Anglican Church. In the years following, life for Catholics in England became very difficult. Some were even martyred, like Bishop John Fisher and Sir Thomas More. By 1540, King Henry had destroyed the thousand-year-old Catholic faith in England and replaced it with something entirely new. The irony is that Queen Anne never gave Henry the son he wanted, only a single daughter. Henry would eventually weary of Anne and have her head chopped off too. He would go through four more wives before dying in 1547.

CHAPTER 23
Trent and the Counter-Reformation

True or False?

1. T
2. T
3. F; He was once called "Defender of the Faith" by the pope because he spoke out against Martin Luther.
4. T
5. F; The Council was called to formulate responses to Protestant objections against the Church and to reform the life and morals of the clergy.
6. F; They were schools for educating priests.
7. T

8. F; He founded a seminary in Milan.
9. T
10. T

Double Puzzle

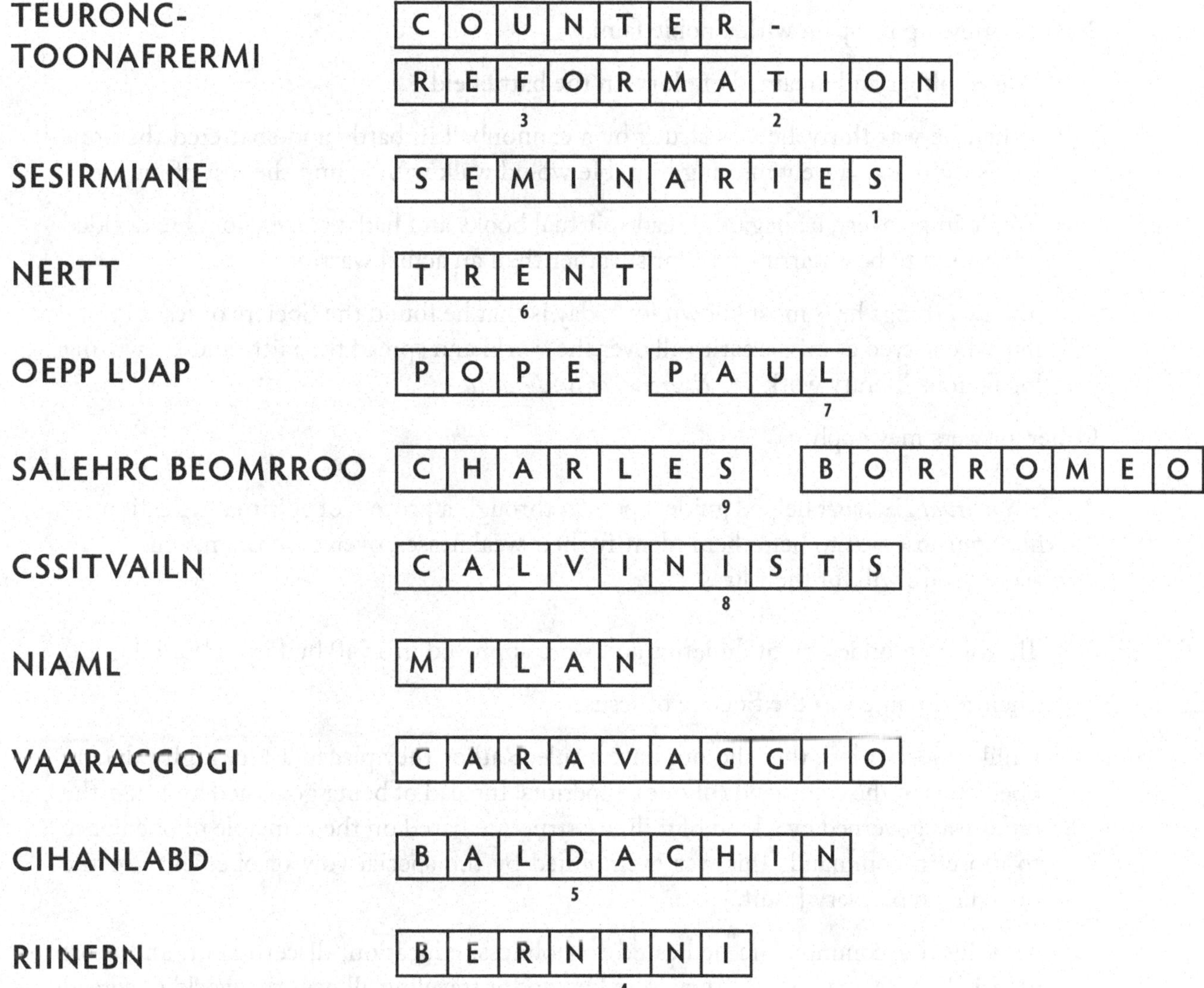

The Capuchin friar and theologian who was sent to preach among the Calvinists of Switzerland to bring them back to the faith, but was eventually martyred.

S	T	.	F	I	D	E	L	I	S
1	2		3	4	5	6	7	8	9

CHAPTER 24

The Jesuits

Short Answer

Answer the following questions in a few complete sentences.

1. • He grew up in Spain with a noble family.

    • Was a soldier and dreamed of glory on the battlefield.

    • When he was thirty, he was struck by a cannonball in battle and shattered the bone in his right leg, gravely injuring him. He would walk with a limp the rest of his life.

    • While in recovery, he began to read spiritual books and had a conversion. He decided he wanted to be a warrior for Christ rather than an actual warrior.

    • The two things he is most known for today is that he found the Society of Jesus (Jesuits), who served as missionaries all over the world and spread the faith, and for writing his famous literary work *The Exercises of St. Ignatius.*

Other answers may apply.

2. *The Spiritual Exercises* helped guide a person through a process of spiritual reflection whose purpose was to help them identify their weaknesses, overcome them, and discern God's will for their lives.

3. • They were founded by St. Ignatius and were approved in 1540 by Pope Paul III.

    • Their real name was the Society of Jesus.

    • Unlike most orders, they did not have a rule. Rather, they placed a very high value on obedience to the commands of one's superiors. Instead of being governed by a rule, the order was governed by a kind of military structure based on the principle of obedience to those in command. This was exemplified by the special vow of obedience to the pope taken by every Jesuit.

    • They lived a common life dedicated to holiness, education, discernment, and most especially missionary work. They were known for traveling all over the world to spread the Gospel.

    • St. Francis Xavier is a famous Jesuit who achieved sainthood.

4. The Penal Laws were a series of anti-Catholic measures Queen Elizabeth of England passed in the sixteenth century. She was the daughter of Henry VIII and Anne Boleyn and was a zealous Protestant. She followed the rule of Queen Mary who was Catholic and sparked a Catholic revival in England during her reign.

After outlawing Catholicism, Pope Pius V excommunicated Elizabeth and said English subjects did not have to obey her. In response, Elizabeth established the Penal Laws. The word *penal* means to penalize or punish. The Penal Laws punished Catholics for remaining loyal to the Church. They made it a crime to convert to Catholicism and forced all English subjects to attend Anglican services or pay a fine. It was also considered treason to print or share the decrees of the pope and made it a capital crime to even be a priest within the kingdom. This meant that any priest caught in England could be executed just for being a priest. All these laws were enforced in Ireland as well.

5. Many heroic Catholics continued to practice their faith. They were able to do this because brave priests came to England to minister to them in secret, risking their lives in the process. Most of them were Englishmen themselves, Catholics who had fled England, entered the priesthood, and returned to their home country to hear confessions and say Mass secretly. Many of these priests were Jesuits.

   Those who were captured—and there were many—could be executed by being hanged, drawn, and quartered. Some of them, like St. Edmund Campion, a Jesuit priest, was martyred and eventually declared a saint. But for most regular Catholics, practicing their faith was mostly a matter of just keeping to themselves – and evading the army of spies Queen Elizabeth had throughout the kingdom searching for Catholic priests.

Word Search

F	N	S	C	E	C	T	I	G	X	P	M	D	N	W	K	G	R
B	R	B	U	U	O	E	Q	K	B	D	V	Y	H	A	P	R	L
X	Z	A	K	I	S	W	I	I	O	X	O	N	H	U	Z	K	T
M	Y	R	N	K	T	D	G	F	P	J	J	T	Z	S	S	W	K
G	I	O	V	C	P	A	Q	R	Q	E	E	Q	F	T	M	O	S
N	B	R	H	I	I	E	N	V	K	J	F	H	N	I	X	C	P
V	J	X	W	H	N	S	X	G	O	L	S	S	P	U	C	B	I
V	L	J	N	D	Z	H	X	I	I	F	R	E	B	S	X	C	J
A	Z	M	C	Q	S	U	I	A	K	G	N	V	R	E	J	U	I
A	C	I	M	R	S	Y	N	H	V	A	F	T	I	J	K	D	A
K	R	S	K	M	V	J	P	K	L	I	R	G	W	U	B	T	U
I	W	S	Y	K	Y	P	H	L	A	H	E	I	I	Q	Q	C	R
S	P	I	R	I	T	U	A	L	E	X	E	R	C	I	S	E	S
X	F	O	N	H	N	W	H	Q	Z	N	E	W	H	A	S	K	I
D	U	N	W	D	S	J	M	A	E	F	T	U	Y	G	U	N	F
C	J	A	M	Q	F	X	R	G	C	Y	T	F	K	L	C	Z	Y
P	S	R	H	T	E	B	A	Z	I	L	E	Y	X	L	G	K	L
L	T	Y	S	M	M	P	D	E	I	T	M	C	X	A	X	J	W

CHAPTER 25
Missions Abroad

Multiple Choice

Pick the best answer.

1. C
2. A
3. B
4. D
5. C
6. A
7. B
8. D
9. A
10. C

Writing Assignment: Converting a Native Tribe

Answers will vary.

CHAPTER 26
Jansenism and Gallicanism

Matching

1. A
2. E
3. C
4. G
5. H
6. B
7. F
8. D

Double Puzzle

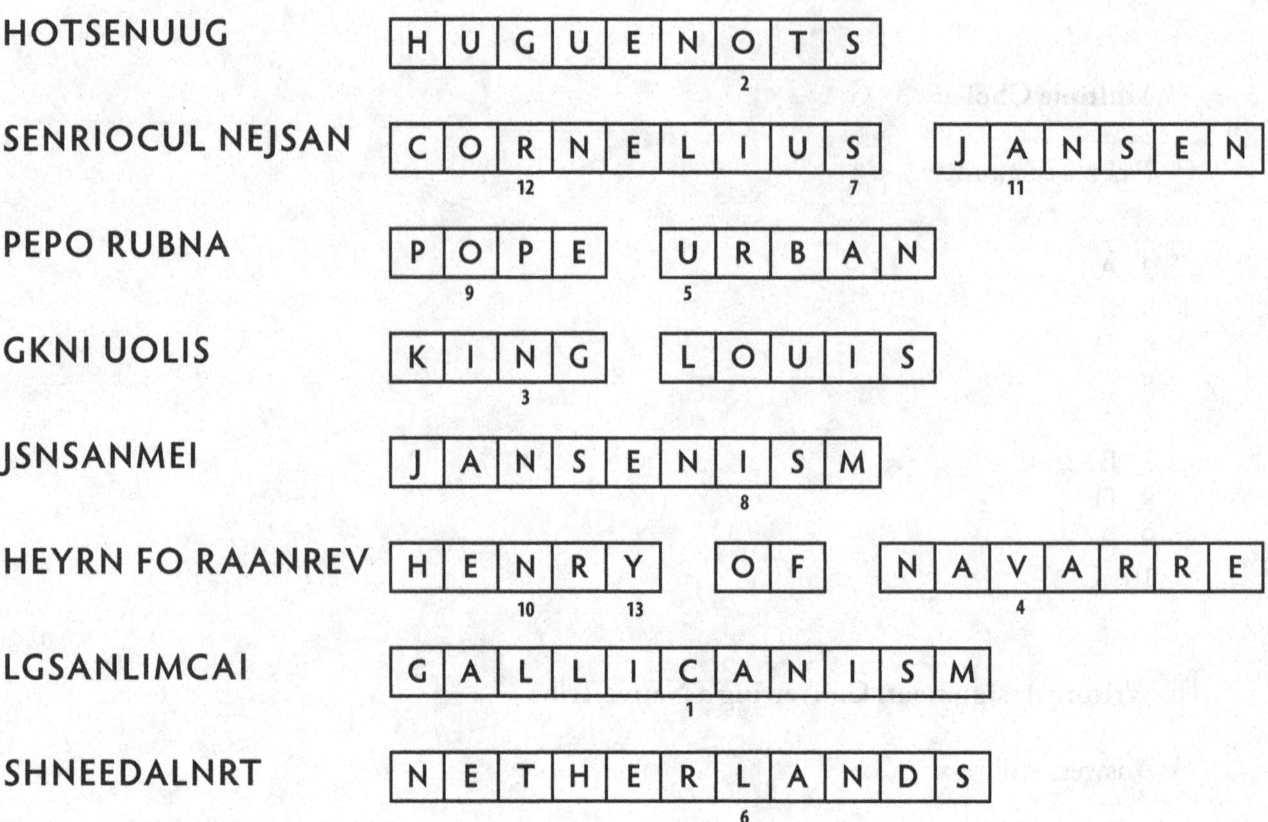

A strange heretical movement originating in Paris that led to bizarre expressions of piety:

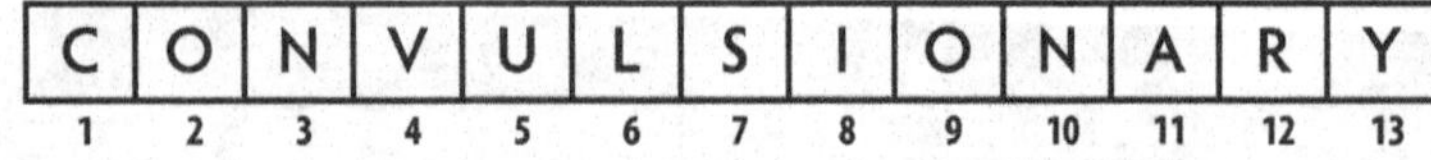

CHAPTER 27

The Age of Revolution

True or False?

1. T
2. F; Some actually gave in to it, including Holy Roman Emperor Joseph II.
3. T
4. F; It was a time of scientific discovery, when many of the principles of modern science were worked out in physics, medicine, astronomy, and other areas.
5. F; The Jesuits were the prime target of anti-clericalists.
6. T
7. F; They were beheaded with the guillotine.
8. F; Maximilien Robespierre led the Committee of Public Safety.

Crossword Puzzle

CHAPTER 28

After the Revolution

Fill in the Blank

1. Pius VII
2. concordat
3. prisoner
4. democratic
5. liberty
6. Jesuits
7. James II
8. Catholic Relief Act
9. John Henry Newman
10. Baltimore

Word Search

E	Z	O	K	V	Z	U	A	N	L	B	Y	T	U	X	R	C
H	I	P	T	Z	W	I	O	W	A	A	M	A	X	L	A	B
M	S	I	L	A	R	E	B	I	L	K	Z	D	Z	T	N	B
H	S	R	V	P	L	C	D	P	U	U	K	R	H	J	B	S
X	M	I	F	O	W	Q	I	X	K	O	Q	O	T	M	N	N
J	A	G	P	P	Z	E	K	T	K	R	L	C	V	J	U	X
H	A	A	B	I	Z	S	U	U	A	I	D	N	N	V	Q	B
T	N	M	O	U	K	L	A	V	C	R	P	O	P	D	P	C
G	Z	Z	E	S	N	N	Y	R	I	G	C	C	H	A	Z	O
W	I	N	Y	S	R	E	E	H	W	L	G	O	Y	P	O	J
N	H	M	W	P	M	L	R	B	V	R	T	A	M	M	G	S
Q	P	N	M	T	I	N	E	W	M	A	N	Z	G	E	X	X
U	H	P	V	E	G	H	L	R	O	C	F	F	A	Y	D	D
F	R	E	F	H	N	U	C	S	R	B	G	C	P	M	N	N
T	F	A	D	O	C	X	H	T	A	X	I	Z	R	G	G	I
N	C	K	G	H	X	Q	Q	Z	G	F	A	V	J	N	O	D
T	T	M	T	P	M	H	I	D	I	K	F	X	V	S	E	W

CHAPTER 29
The Age of Pius IX

Short Answer

1. The Catholic Church knew it had to decide how to respond to the spread of liberal thinking. Cardinals debated whether the Church should take a hard line against the rising tide of liberalism or be more sympathetic to it. In the papal conclave of 1846, the cardinals elected Giovanni Maria Mastai Ferretti, the bishop of Imola, who took the name Pius IX. As bishop of Imola, Ferretti was known as a friend to the liberal reforms sweeping across Europe. The cardinals who elected him thought perhaps as pope he would help reconcile the Church to the new mood of the age. When liberal revolutions broke out across Europe, however, including within the Papal States themselves, Pius grew skeptical towards the liberal movements. He began to see liberalism and the Church as enemies, between whom no truce was possible.

2. Pius IX was not going to allow this to happen without a fight. He formed an international force of Catholic volunteers called the Zouaves to defend the Papal States. The Zouaves came from all over the Catholic world to fight for Pius IX. The papal army was passionate, but they were still small. This forced Pius to turn to Napoleon Bonaparte III, who had become first president and then emperor of the French in 1852. Napoleon kept French troops stationed in the Papal States to help Pius IX and the Zouaves fight off the Italian army. The French and Zouaves would go on to fight many battles against the Italians, the most famous at the Italian village of Mentana.

3. Pius knew he could not win a battle against Emmanuel's forces, so the shots were more symbolic in nature. He didn't want the people to think he was inviting the Italian forces in; he wanted them to know he did not agree with the occupation of Rome. The shots were signals of his opposition.

4. King Victor Emmanuel's government shut down monasteries and convents and the Jesuits were expelled from the kingdom. Many Church lands were confiscated, laws were passed making it difficult to send children to religious schools, and Victor Emmanuel pressured Pius to renounce his claims to the Papal States.

5. Pius IX was known first and foremost for standing strong in the face of so much liberal persecution and violence. He defended the Church in many ways during this troubling time period. He also summoned the First Vatican Council, which taught many things, including papal infallibility. He also defined the dogma of the Immaculate Conception, stating that Mary was conceived without any stain of sin. Pope Pius IX died in 1878 as one of the longest reigning popes in history. He was later beatified and today is known as Blessed Pius IX.

Writing Assignment: Explaining the Immaculate Conception

Answers will vary.

CHAPTER 30
A New Century With New Challenges

Multiple Choice

Pick the best answer.

1. B
2. D
3. A
4. B
5. C
6. D
7. D
8. C
9. B
10. A

Writing Assignment: Living the Little Way

Answers will vary.

CHAPTER 31
Under Fascism and Communism

Matching

1. N
2. A
3. H
4. K
5. L
6. E
7. F
8. J
9. G
10. C
11. B
12. I
13. M
14. D

Double Puzzle

Scrambled	Answer	Numbered letters
FMATAI	F A T I M A	M = 1
SRCTIOSRE	C R I S T E R O S	I = 2
GOTRLPAU	P O R T U G A L	A = 4, L = 6
CULIA	L U C I A	C = 5
TISFSASC	F A S C I S T S	F = 9
MMCOTINSUS	C O M M U N I S T S	O = 8, U = 14, N = 15
SPUI	P I U S	S = 13
MUGLEI ROP	M I G U E L P R O	E = 12, R = 3
RONSIPRAETA	R E P A R A T I O N S	E = 7
HET RETGA AWR	T H E G R E A T W A R	H = 11, T = 10

Took place on October 13, 1917:

CHAPTER 32

The Church in the Second World War

1. Nazis
2. Jewish
3. encyclical
4. concentration camps
5. Catholics
6. St. Maximilian Kolbe; Auschwitz
7. Pope Pius XII
8. committing suicide

Word Search

C	R	Z	N	T	E	H	Z	C	P	I	R	H	F	G	J	I
S	O	H	H	B	Z	A	Y	T	J	T	H	E	J	C	F	F
S	P	N	L	E	H	Z	T	Z	E	N	V	Y	L	X	V	Q
T	B	O	C	Y	N	A	M	R	E	G	T	U	N	T	G	B
O	K	R	Y	E	Y	M	J	J	C	V	D	Z	X	W	I	S
O	T	Y	Y	K	N	C	N	A	R	S	A	U	T	O	W	H
W	J	W	I	I	M	T	U	J	R	I	V	R	B	R	A	B
P	S	C	S	Z	N	S	R	W	G	Z	L	J	W	L	W	A
Q	I	Z	I	B	C	G	S	A	T	A	C	T	V	D	Y	E
S	Q	S	O	H	S	L	Y	E	T	N	D	V	Z	W	S	Y
L	G	U	W	P	I	U	S	O	O	I	I	O	L	A	N	Q
C	M	I	R	W	U	Q	S	I	W	G	O	P	U	R	K	E
M	T	J	J	M	Z	R	D	G	T	K	Z	N	Q	I	E	Z
Z	D	C	K	K	R	G	R	O	G	K	U	T	C	I	L	V
V	F	V	Y	F	D	Y	Z	A	A	W	X	J	V	A	U	G
K	A	V	P	A	F	H	G	J	Q	Y	V	G	J	T	M	N
Y	F	T	J	E	M	D	U	L	K	R	N	K	J	K	O	P

CHAPTER 33
The Second Vatican Council

True or False?

1. F; Mass attendance was low.
2. F; In parts of Africa and Asia, there were many conversions.
3. F; It was not meant to change the Church's teachings but to change the way they were delivered and explained to the faithful.
4. T
5. T
6. F; It was the "New Order of the Mass."
7. F; It changed much of the Mass to the vernacular of the country where the Mass was being held, but parts of the Mass remained in Latin.
8. T

Writing Assignment – Comparing and Contrasting the Old Rite and the Novus Ordo

Answers will vary.

CHAPTER 34
Hopes and Fears

Multiple Choice

Pick the best answer.

1. C
2. A
3. D
4. C
5. A

Crossword Puzzle

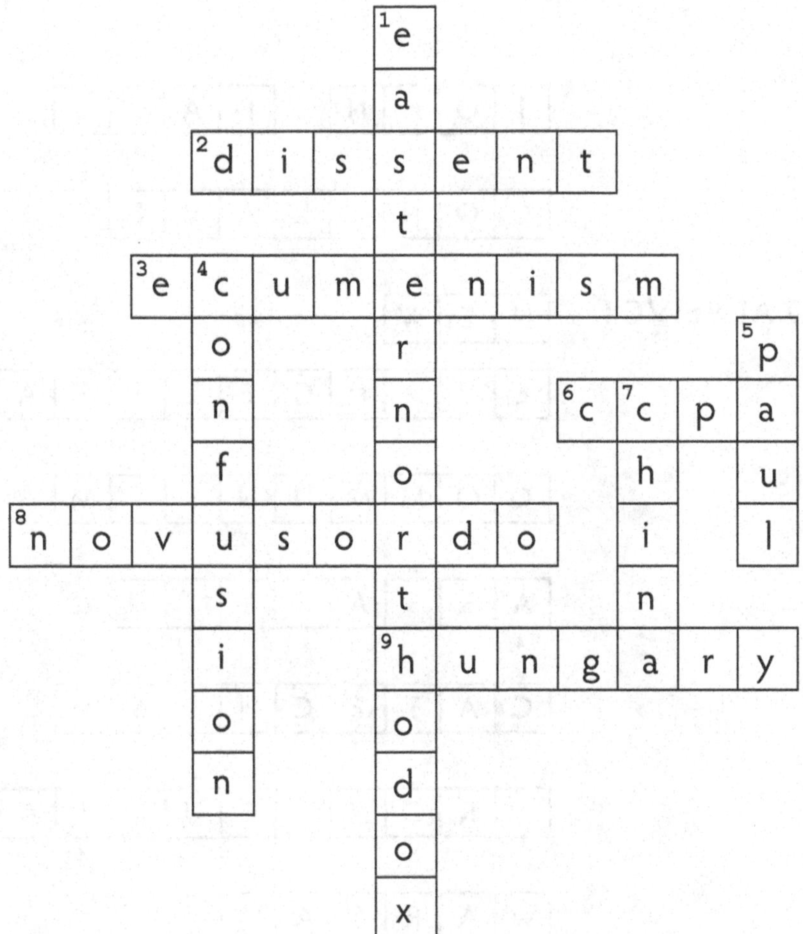

CHAPTER 35

The Pontificate of Pope St. John Paul II

Fill in the Blank

1. John Paul
2. Poland
3. non-Italian
4. May 13
5. *Catechism of the Catholic Church*
6. new evangelization

Double Puzzle

JNOH LPAU	J O(8) H N P A U L
EVCOCANL	C O N C L A V E
WEN IONEAZALNEIVGT	N E W(3) E V A N G(7) E L I Z A T I O N
MUNCOMMIS	C O M M U N(5) I S M
SAINSSSA	A(4) S S A S S I N
TIESCCAHM	C A T E(2) C H I S M
IONR RUCNITA	I R O N C U R T(6) A I N
WRWAAS	W A R S A W(1)
CAALINRD	C A R D(9) I N A L

At John Paul II's famous Mass in Poland, the people chanted this.

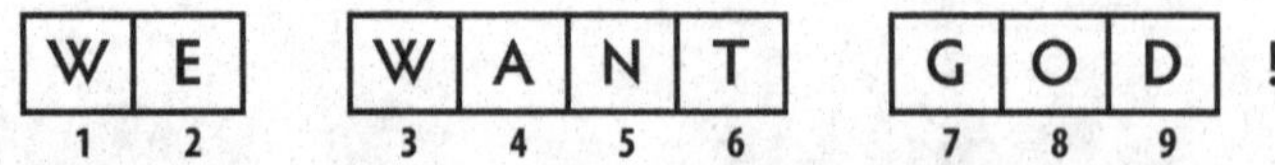

CHAPTER 36
The Church in the Twenty-First Century

Writing Assignment: Looking Back

Answers will vary.

Writing Assignment: Looking Ahead

Answers will vary.